WORLD RELIGIONS
SIKHISM
THIRD EDITION

WORLD RELIGIONS

African Traditional Religion
Baha'i Faith
Buddhism
Catholicism & Orthodox Christianity
Confucianism
Daoism
Hinduism
Islam
Judaism
Native American Religions
Protestantism
Shinto
Sikhism
Zoroastrianism

WORLD RELIGIONS
SIKHISM
THIRD EDITION

by
Nikky-Guninder Kaur Singh
Series Editors: Joanne O'Brien and Martin Palmer

CHELSEA HOUSE
PUBLISHERS
An imprint of Infobase Publishing

Sikhism, Third Edition

Chelsea House
An imprint of Infobase Publishing
132 West 31st Street
New York NY 10001

Library of Congress Cataloging-in-Publication Data
Singh, Nikky-Guninder Kaur.
  Sikhism / by Nikky-Guninder Kaur Singh. —3rd ed.
      p. cm. — (World religions)
  Previously published: 2004.
  Includes bibliographical references and index.
  ISBN 978-1-60413-114-7
  1. Sikhism—Juvenile literature. I. Title.
  BL2018.S5175 2009
  294.6—dc22
                        2008029662

Chelsea House books are available at special discounts when purchased in bulk quantities for businesses, associations, institutions, or sales promotions. Please call our Special Sales Department in New York at (212) 967-8800 or (800) 322-8755.

You can find Chelsea House on the World Wide Web at http://www.chelseahouse.com

This book was produced for Chelsea House by Bender Richardson White, Uxbridge, U.K.
Project Editor: Lionel Bender
Text Editor: Ronne Randall
Designer: Ben White
Picture Researchers: Joanne O'Brien and Kim Richardson
Maps and symbols: Stefan Chabluk

Printed in China

CP BRW 10 9 8 7 6 5 4 3 2 1
This book is printed on acid-free paper.

All links and Web addresses were checked and verified to be correct at the time of publication. Because of the dynamic nature of the Web, some addresses and links may have changed since publication and may no longer be valid.

CONTENTS

PREFACE

Almost from the start of civilization, more than 10,000 years ago, religion has shaped human history. Today more than half the world's population practice a major religion or indigenous spiritual tradition. In many 21st-century societies, including the United States, religion still shapes people's lives and plays a key role in politics and culture. And in societies throughout the world increasing ethnic and cultural diversity has led to a variety of religions being practiced side by side. This makes it vital that we understand as much as we can about the world's religions.

The World Religions series, of which this book is a part, sets out to achieve this aim. It is written and designed to appeal to both students and general readers. The books offer clear, accessible overviews of the major religious traditions and institutions of our time. Each volume in the series describes where a particular religion is practiced, its origins and history, its central beliefs and important rituals, and its contributions to world civilization. Carefully chosen photographs complement the text, and sidebars, a map, fact file, glossary, bibliography, and index are included to help readers gain a more complete understanding of the subject at hand.

These books will help clarify what religion is all about and reveal both the similarities and differences in the great spiritual traditions practiced around the world today.

Sikh Populations

Majority Sikh population

Large Sikh population

Widespread Sikh population

Small or no Sikh population

CHAPTER 1

INTRODUCTION: SIKHISM AND THE MODERN WORLD

The Sikh religion is one of the youngest of all world religions. It began about 500 years ago in the Punjab region of India. Most of its followers still live in this fertile region, which is located in the foothills of the Himalaya Mountains in northwest India and east Pakistan.

In all there are about 24 million Sikhs in the world today and around 16 million of them live in the Indian part of Punjab. At Partition in 1947, when the new state of Pakistan was created and the area of the Punjab was split between two countries, many Sikhs moved across the border to live in the Indian area of the Punjab. About 8 million Sikhs are spread in other parts of India and beyond. There are Sikh populations in England, Scotland, the United States, Canada, Pakistan, East Africa, the Arab Emirates, Iran, Malaysia, and Hong Kong.

Although Sikhs represent only about 2 percent of India's huge population, they are highly visible. What makes them dominant in society is their strong work ethic, which is part of their religion, and their courageousness. A large proportion of India's military officers are Sikhs, as are many of its army troops and many of its

Harimandir, the House of God, in Amritsar, India, is the most sacred of all Sikh holy places. It is also known as the Golden Temple and rises above a reflecting pool, the "pool of nectar," built by Guru Ram Das in 1577. Work on the Harimandir itself was completed in 1601.

airline pilots. Sikhs are also known to be fine athletes, and many have represented India on Olympic teams.

Sikhs may be found in cities and towns the world over, where they have settled in search of work and education. In most metropolitan areas one can find Sikh professors, lawyers, accountants and doctors, taxi drivers and shopkeepers, students, mechanics, and office workers. They are especially significant in the world of business. During the race between the United States and the former Soviet Union to put the first person on the moon in the 1950s and 1960s, Sikhs in their far-flung communities joked that whoever reached the moon first would find a Sikh already there.

It is fairly easy to recognize a traditional Sikh. Every Sikh man's second name is Singh, meaning "lion" or "lionhearted." Every Sikh woman's second name is Kaur, meaning "princess." Both men and women wear a steel bracelet around the right wrist as an emblem of their faith. Sikh men can often be identified by their beards and by the turban, a headdress that consists of a long length of colorful cloth wrapped around the head. Such a visible symbol has sometimes been a problem. Britain had to pass special laws to exempt turbaned Sikhs from a law requiring them to wear motorcycle helmets. In the United States a still-unresolved court case brought by a Sikh has led the U.S. Army to consider whether its Sikhs may be permitted to wear the turban with their uniforms.

WHAT IS SIKHISM?

The fundamental principle of Sikhism is, "There is only One Being and Truth is its Name"—in Punjabi, *Ikk oan kar sat nam.* Sikhs believe in the Divine One, the Supreme Ultimate Reality through which the universe was created and continues to exist. Because of this belief scholars usually consider Sikhism to be a monotheistic religion. For Sikhs the Supreme Ultimate Reality cannot be seen or represented visually in a picture or a statue. It transcends all space, time, and gender. It takes in all other gods and beliefs. Thus the Sikh ideal includes all religions, races, and cultural backgrounds.

The turban is the most notable feature of Sikh men's clothing. Other men of India may wear the turban, often a feature of Muslim dress, but it is particularly associated with Sikhs who wear it to cover uncut hair, one of the symbols of belonging to the Khalsa, or Sikh brotherhood.

Sikhism arises from the teachings of Guru Nanak, the first guru, or teacher, who is believed to have been divinely inspired. Nanak was followed by nine other gurus, all of whom are revered as great teachers and leaders. The words of the gurus are preserved in Sikh scripture, the Guru Granth, the sacred volume that includes the poems and songs of the gurus. Sikhs turn to this holy book for inspiration and guidance in ritual and worship, and they treat it with the highest respect. It is at the center of all Sikh services and celebrations.

"TRUE LIVING"

Sikhs reject ritual and external forms of religion. They focus instead on living their faith. Fellowship, community, and family life are at the center of Sikhism. Sikhs consider other Sikhs to be their brothers and sisters, as well as those from other faiths, including those from Islam. Sikh travelers to other countries often consult telephone books for Sikh names and then call, knowing that they will be welcomed as family. Marriage and children are extremely important to Sikhs. Infidelity is forbidden.

Sikhs do not use tobacco products or any intoxicants, both of which they believe harm the mind. Yet early Sikh gurus rejected the idea that self-denial is necessary to the high ideal of what they called "true living." In India, a country of many vegetarians, a significant number of Sikhs eat meat. They enjoy singing, games, and sports events, and their holidays have a festival atmosphere. Wherever Sikhs live they are involved citizens, working hard and playing hard and trying to live up to the ideals of their faith.

THE ORIGINS OF SIKHISM

Sikhs trace their religion to Guru Nanak, a leader whose title, *guru*, means "teacher," or "one who enlightens." The India into which Nanak was born was home to both Hinduism and Islam. Hin-

THE IDEALS OF SIKHISM

Worship of the One Ultimate Reality—Sikhs worship what is to them the Ultimate Reality, the timeless, formless force that is above all things and present in all things. They take seriously the words of the scripture to "rejoice in My Name." People may pray anywhere at any time, but many Sikhs feel that at dawn and dusk they can more easily focus their minds on the Ultimate One. Morning and evening prayers are offered in the *gurdwara,* or Sikh house of worship.

Dignity of labor—Earning one's living by honest work and working hard for one's livelihood are good deeds that earn merit toward a better life now and in the future. Sikhs do not look down on any kind of work. They find laziness or living off others unacceptable.

Equality of all people—All people are equal because the Divine is present in everyone. Sikhs reject all distinctions of social class, race, and creed because they are artificial and because they separate people from the One Ultimate Reality. Men and women have an equal voice. Everyone is welcome to participate in the life of the Sikh community; no one is excluded.

Service—Sikhs express their beliefs through service to the One by reading from the scriptures and helping with the upkeep of the *gurdwara.* They also serve the Sikh community by helping fellow Sikhs as brothers and sisters. Finally they share the fruits of their labor with the disadvantaged outside the Sikh community, giving both money and time to charity.

Community—Fellowship is an act of faith. Sikhs everywhere consider themselves to be a family united through the grace of the Ultimate Reality. They join together regularly for worship and for community meals and activities. They freely extend hospitality and aid to other Sikhs, both friends and strangers.

duism had originated on the banks of India's Indus River many centuries before, and Islam had come to India from Saudi Arabia between the 11th and 13th centuries C.E.

Following worship, members of a congregation join in preparing food in the *gurdwara* kitchens to serve at *langar,* the Sikh community meal. The *langar* is free and is open to people of all beliefs and backgrounds.

EXPLORATION AND REVIVAL

Nanak was born in 1469 C.E. At the time Europe was experiencing the Renaissance, a time of revival and progress in art, literature, and the sciences. In 1466 the Gutenberg Bible, the first book known to be printed in the Western world, marked the appearance of movable type. This invention spread literacy to an ever wider audience. At the same time European explorers were voyaging to parts of the world that were unknown on their home continent. In 1492 Christopher Columbus sailed from Spain to search for a westward route to Asia and reached the shores of America. Six years later the Portuguese explorer Vasco da Gama left Lisbon, sailed around the continent of Africa, and landed on the Arabian seacoast in the Malabar region of southern India.

IMPULSE FOR A NEW RELIGION

The world of religion, too, was changing. In both East and West, Asia and Europe, people were asking questions: What is the basis of religion? Has this basis been lost over time? Have ritual and ceremony taken the place of faith and devotion? Religious thinkers worried that religion had been reduced to a hollow shell of external form and practice. Fundamentals in religion were being challenged, faults were becoming apparent, and religious leaders were emerging who were reviving old traditions or developing new ones. In Germany Martin Luther (1483–1546) challenged the teachings of the Christian Church and set in motion the wheels of the Reformation, a movement that led to Protestantism. In India Luther's contemporary Guru Nanak provided the impulse for a new and vital religious tradition.

GOD AS THE ONLY REALITY

By 1500, when Nanak began teaching, both Hinduism and Islam had enriched Indian thought with their devotional literature, art, and spirituality. Many scholars find traces of both Hinduism and Islam in Sikhism. They point in particular to echoes of the work of Kabir (1440–1518). Both poet and religious reformer, Kabir drew together aspects of the Hindu Bhakti movement and Islamic

Sufism. The Hindu Bhaktas stressed the belief that God is the only reality, and they rejected the rigid social structures and rituals of other forms of Hinduism. The Muslim Sufis were mystics who believed in merging the individual self with the One Universal Being. Sikhism shares these elements and indeed it has similarities to Christianity, Buddhism, and Daoism as well. However for the Sikhs Nanak was clearly the founder of a separate and distinct religious tradition, the first of a line of gurus who underscored his special understanding.

THE GURU GRANTH

The leadership of Guru Nanak passed successively to nine other gurus, each of whom became in turn a spiritual leader of the Sikhs. The guruship was always based on merit, fitness, dedication, and capability, breaking with Hindu tradition that the eldest son should succeed his father.

In 1604 the fifth guru, Arjan, compiled a *granth*, a "book" or "sacred volume." In it he collected the poems and songs of the earlier gurus and added his own to the collection. He also included the works of several Muslim and Hindu holy men such as Kabir. A little over 100 years later, in 1708, the 10th guru, Gobind Singh, decreed that from then on, there would be no living gurus. The *granth* would be the only guru. Since then, the focus of Sikh ritual and worship has been the Guru Granth. Sikh ceremonies relating to birth, initiation, marriage, and death take place in its presence.

THE FIVE KS

Of the five symbols prescribed for the Khalsa by Gobind Singh, the most important was *kesha,* or "hair," which was to remain uncut to provide a distinct identity. Thus Sikhs allow their hair and beards to grow unshorn. The other four symbols were *kangha,* or "comb," for neatness; *kara,* a steel "bracelet" to be worn on the right arm as a symbol of strength and the unbroken circle of Oneness; *kaccha,* or "drawers," a pair of loose shorts worn as an undergarment; and *kirpan,* or "sword," a symbol of self-defense and the fight against injustice. These external signs of Sikh faith are known as the *five Ks* and are now worn by all Sikhs, both men and women.

SIKHS AND MILITANCY

Early in their history the Sikhs were forced by religious persecution, and by the execution of two of their gurus by Muslim rulers, to arm themselves for protection. In 1699

Guru Gobind Singh organized an elite fighting force, the Khalsa or "Pure Ones." The members of the Khalsa swore to have faith in the One Reality, to consider all human beings equal, regardless of their religion or social level, and to help the poor and defend the faith. Gobind Singh gave the first five members of the Khalsa the second name Singh to signify their equality. He also announced the five symbols that would mark them as members of the Khalsa, thus distinguishing them from non-Sikhs. These are known as the *five Ks*.

Sikh troops played an important and active role during the period of the British Empire. In this photograph they are in South Africa as part of the British forces fighting in the Boer War (1889–1902).

SIKHS AND THE BRITISH EMPIRE

The Sikh fighting forces have had a long and proud history of military discipline and courage in battle. They remained undefeated until the mid-1800s, when India came under the rule of the British Empire. A period of relative calm followed, during which the Sikhs lived peacefully in the Punjab. Under British rule many Sikhs acquired land and the area prospered.

Sikhs fought as part of the British Army in World War I (1914–18) and achieved distinction. After the war, however, disputes about control of Sikh holy places caused unrest. In 1919 the British denied Sikhs permission to gather for a New Year festival. When the Sikhs refused to obey the British fired on them, killing hundreds. In 1925 matters improved slightly when the government gave Sikhs a voice in the management of their own shrines. A period of uneasy peace followed until World War II (1939–45), when the Sikhs again fought alongside the British, again with honor.

PARTITION, TENSION, AND NEW CHALLENGES

After World War II the British left India, and as part of the general decolonization agreement a new country, Pakistan, was carved out which absorbed most of the Punjab. More than 2.5 million Sikhs found themselves in a Muslim country that did not want them. They were forced to leave their homes and move over the border to less desirable land in India. The discontent that resulted eventually led to a movement for a separate Sikh state. By the early 1980s tensions between the Indian government and the Sikh separatists had worsened to the point of violence. In 1984 a large band of Sikh separatists took refuge in the Golden Temple, one of the Sikh holy places. The Indian Army attacked them there, killing several thousand Sikhs and seriously damaging the temple compound.

The violation of the Golden Temple remains a painful memory for many Sikhs. Tensions eased in the 1990s due to significant political and economic changes affecting Sikhs and all Indians. Sikhs are still seeking justice, equality, and freedom, especially as these values relate to rectifying the abuses of the Indian central government. Members of the *panth* or community are also working for improved economic conditions, infrastructure, and education. The new century presents challenges both old and new for the community. In resisting oppression and fighting for tolerance Sikhs are being true to the teachings of God and of their gurus—all humans possess the Divine spark.

SAHAJ—TRANQUILLITY

Despite the image of militancy that has followed them the Sikhs' message is one of universal love and peace. The concept of *sahaj*, or tranquillity, is central to Guru Nanak's view of the world.

For those who cultivate it, *sahaj* creates an inner peace and points the way to union with the transcendent reality, the One of Sikhism. At the same time it creates an outer good will and leads the individual along paths of peaceful interaction with others. The Hindu ideal of *shanti*, the Jewish ideal of shalom, and the Islamic ideal of salaam are all included in the Sikh yearning for *sahaj*. The search for *sahaj* is part of the quest for peace and the Ultimate.

Sikhs today continue to believe in the Universal Oneness of all Reality and in the equality of all people. Their message of human fellowship amid diversity of race, culture, and belief is an important one for the modern world.

CHAPTER 2

GURU NANAK AND THE ORIGINS OF THE SIKH FAITH

N anak was the first guru of the Sikh religion. Nanak showed people a new way of understanding the Ultimate Reality, the Divine One of the universe. His vision became the way of life for the Sikhs.

Nanak was born on November 29, 1469, in Talwandi, a small Indian village in what is now Pakistan. At the time of Nanak's birth India was ruled by the Muslims. Nanak's family, however, was Hindu. Indian society was organized according to the caste system, a rigid system of social, political, and economic order. A caste is a social group whose members' rank in society is determined by birth. The castes in India ranged from the Brahmins, who were priests and scholars, down to a group whose rank in society was so low that its people were known as untouchables (they prefer to call themselves *Dalit*).

Praying in a Sikh temple or *gurdwara* in Ahmedabad, India. Every *gurdwara* has a copy of the Guru Granth, the Sikh holy scriptures, in the shrine room. These scriptures are considered the 11th and final guru.

Nanak was born into one of the higher castes—the Khatri, or warrior caste. He was named after his older sister, Nanaki. His father was an accountant for the local Muslim landlord. Nanak's mother was known as a pious and gentle woman. By Nanak's lifetime the tradition of keeping written records was well established in Europe and Asia. Thus there are many contemporary accounts of Nanak's life and teachings from people who actually saw and heard him.

JANAMSAKHI, THE BIRTH STORY

In the 16th century, not long after Nanak's passing, his followers wrote short narratives about his birth and life. These narratives, or stories, are the first works of prose in Punjabi, the language of the Punjab, and they are called *Janamsakhi,* from the Punjabi words *janam,* which means "birth," and *sakhi,* which means "story." The writers came from different traditions and social groups, but they all believed that Nanak's life was unique.

The family priest (*harbalish*) had predicted that the newborn child, Nanak, would be a great seer, or prophet:

Both Hindus and Muslims will venerate him. His name will become known on earth and in heaven. The ocean will give him way: so will the earth and the sky. He will worship only one Formless God and teach others to do so. He will hold all men equal as God's creation.
—the Janamsakhi

His early life was marked by the conflicts between Muslims and Hindus. Yet even as a child Nanak was spreading peace and goodwill. The *Janamsakhi* stories record that both Hindus and Muslims were impressed with the boy.

A PROMISING STUDENT

When Nanak was seven years old his father took him first to the Hindu priest of the village to begin his education and then to a school run by a Hindu teacher. For a while Nanak also attended

Guru Nanak, the first of 11 Sikh gurus, with Mardana the musician and Bhai Bala the poet, his beloved disciples who accompanied him on his travels.

a school kept by a Muslim teacher. The boy proved to be an uncommonly bright, enthusiastic, and promising student. His teachers were surprised at his ability to grasp difficult ideas. Soon teachers from both Hindu and Muslim traditions came to realize that there was nothing further they could teach him.

One of the features of the Hindu religion is a belief in reincarnation, or earthly rebirth, to increasingly higher levels of existence. Someone from a low caste may hope that his or her actions in the present will allow rebirth to a higher caste in his or her next life. The person will carry out religious duties to be rewarded in this way. Someone from a high caste is believed to be twice-born—that is, to have gone through a cycle of birth and death. Hindu males from the upper castes wear a "sacred thread," a cord that symbolizes rebirth and distinguishes them from the Untouchables. Each caste has different quality thread to signify the caste.

NANAK'S EXTRAORDINARY LIFE

According to the *Janamsakhi* stories, Nanak, like all Hindu boys, was required at an early age to participate in an initiation ritual in which he would put on the sacred thread. When the priest called on him he refused, because even at that very early age Nanak was opposed to ritual and to the caste system that limited the freedom of people in his society. In a time when many Hindus and Muslims were focusing on external ceremony and ritual, Nanak was inclined toward the life of the spirit.

Nanak lost interest in formal education. He left his tutors and turned his attention to contemplating the Divine. However where others perceived the spark of divinity, Nanak's father saw only a teenager who would not attend school. Wanting the boy to make himself useful, he sent Nanak to the fields to graze cattle. Soon the village of Talwandi was abuzz with accounts of Nanak the herder having the power to work miracles when a field of wheat that had been eaten by cattle had miraculously grown again that same day.

On another occasion Nanak lay down one summer day to rest under a tree. He fell asleep. The sun slowly rose to its highest point and the shade of the tree retreated, leaving the sleeping Nanak exposed to the direct rays of the scorching midday sun. While Nanak slept a cobra, one of India's deadliest snakes, slid from a nearby hole. It spread its hood to shade Nanak's face from the burning sun. A town official observed the event, and marveling at what he had seen, carried the news back to the townspeople.

These stories and others from the *Janamsakhi* portray the extraordinary dimension of Nanak's life. The simple narratives illustrate his religious and ethical teachings. They also incorporate verses from his poems and songs. Sikhs both young and old read and retell the *Janamsakhi* stories. In many Sikh households parents and grandparents read these stories to young children at bedtime.

A Miracle from God

A *Janamsakhi* story says that one day while he was grazing the cattle, Nanak sat on the ground, rapt in the beauty of nature and deep in meditation. The cattle he was supposed to be watching strayed into a neighbor's wheat field and quickly devoured the crop. The farmer was enraged. He angrily complained to the village chief and soon a delegation came to assess the damage. To their amazement not a blade of wheat was gone, and "the field seemed to proclaim that if any damage had been done, it must be elsewhere." The farmer had seen with his own eyes the chomping cattle in the midst of the ruined crop. Now he saw his crop perfectly restored. He humbly admitted that a miracle of God had taken place.

NANAK'S DIVINE CALLING

When he was a young man Nanak moved to the city of Sultanpur to live with his sister Nanaki and her husband. In the city he

A 16th-century painting of Guru Nanak with his disciple Mardana and King Shivanath of Jaffna, Sri Lanka. Guru Nanak is sitting in the center, holding prayer-beads, and his companion Mardana holds a mandolin. King Shivanath is listening to Guru Nanak's spiritual teachings with his hands together in a gesture of devotion. This painting depicts one of the many extensive journeys that Guru Nanak made to teach and to spread his message of reaching the Divine.

worked in a store owned by the local Muslim landlord, and to the landlord's dismay he often gave away goods without charging for them. Yet Nanak's generosity did not deplete the store's supplies. When Nanak was called to account for his actions, it was found that nothing was missing.

One morning, as was his custom, Nanak went to bathe in the River Bein. When he did not return, his family and friends began to search for him. His clothes were found on the riverbank but there was no sign of the young man anywhere. Everyone believed that he had drowned in the river. Nanak was beloved by all and the entire city was plunged into gloom.

On the third day Nanak returned. He explained that during his absence he had been in direct communion with the Ultimate Reality, the Divine One.

NANAK'S MESSAGE

When Nanak first emerged from the river he pronounced the words that would form the foundation of Sikhism: "There is no Hindu; there is no Muslim." Thus, in one sentence, Nanak rejected all religious and sectarian distinctions among human beings. The statement does not deny the variety and richness of religious beliefs. Rather it embraces them all and celebrates the shared basis of all humanity. The vision of the Infinite One enabled Nanak to recognize the unity of society beyond narrow categories such as Hindu and Muslim, or for that matter, Jew, Christian, or Buddhist. His encounter with the Divine had showed him that all religions taught one true message—that of devotion to the One Reality.

NANAK'S VISION

The *Janamsakhi* recounts Nanak's vision of the Divine after he had been missing for three days:

As the Almighty willed, Nanak the devotee was ushered into the Divine Presence. Then a cup filled with amrita (nectar) was given him with the command, "Nanak, this is the cup of Name-Adoration. Drink it . . . I am with you and I do bless and exalt you. Whoever remembers you will have my favor. Go, rejoice, in My Name, and teach others to do so . . . I have bestowed upon you the gift of My Name. Let this be your calling." Nanak offered his salutations and stood up.

Nanak experienced the Ultimate Reality as without form and transcendent, above all things. He did not actually see the Ultimate Reality in any concrete form. He heard the divine words, the cup of nectar appeared before him, and he drank from it. Thus began the Sikh religion. This account portrays Nanak's revelation as unique but one that his followers can also experience for themselves.

TRAVEL AND TEACHING

Nanak set out to teach this message of the One Reality and the one fellowship of humanity. He was then in his twenties, married to a woman named Sulakhani, and the father of two sons, Sri Chand and Lakhmi Chand. The call to spread the Divine Word was strong in him and for the next 25 years his travels took him not only throughout India but also to such faraway places as Iraq and Saudi Arabia and even to Mecca, the holy city of Islam.

Bhai Gurdas, an uncle of the fifth guru, Guru Arjan, and a highly esteemed Sikh historian and poet, records that Nanak visited the Hindus, Muslims, and Buddhists and discussed with them their respective scriptures and philosophies. Wherever Nanak went he taught an inner way of reaching the Divine. He exhorted people to discard external rituals and ceremonies. He did not ask others to renounce their religious faith, because to him it did not matter whether they were Hindu or Muslim. The important thing was that they believed in the One Reality and were kind to all.

Nanak's *Sishyas*

Nanak's teaching drew people from different religions, cultures, and levels of society. Wherever he went people began to follow him, won over by his simple, direct manner and his liberal, universal message. These followers came to be known as *sishyas,* the word in the Sanskrit language for "disciples," and eventually came to be called *Sikhs.* To this day people in Tibet worship Guru Nanak by a different name and many Muslims and Hindus recognize Nanak's divine powers.

A COMMUNITY OF DISCIPLES

At the end of his travels Nanak settled on the right bank of the River Ravi in the Punjab. There he founded a village called Kartarpur. A community of disciples grew around him there, but its members did not take vows or live as monks and nuns. The community was a fellowship of men and women engaged in the ordinary occupations of life but devoted to the teachings of Nanak. So from its earliest beginnings Sikhism was both a religion and a way of life, extending to all phases of human conduct. Nanak spent his twilight years working as a farmer in the fields. Sikhs have always emphasized that everyone must work for their living—even gurus.

Nanak was accompanied on his journeys by Mardana, a Muslim family servant and musician,
who played the *rebec,* a three-stringed musical instrument, while Nanak composed and sang
songs full of love for the Divine One. Mardana put Nanak's songs to music
and the two organized community singing.

THE ELEMENTS OF SIKHISM

At Kartarpur Nanak established three important elements of Sikh religious and social discipline: *seva*, *langar*, and *sangat*. These elements have been strong factors in encouraging the Sikh values of equality, fellowship, and humility and in affirming a sense of "familyhood."

SEVA

Seva is voluntary manual labor in the service of the community. It is the performance of a deed of love and selfless service that contributes the work of one's hands to serving fellow human beings both within and outside the Sikh community. *Seva* is the highest ideal in Sikh ethics. Through *seva* Sikh believers cultivate humility, overcome ego, and purify their bodies and minds. *Seva* is an essential condition of spiritual discipline. Nanak taught that "by practicing deeds of humble and devoted service alone does one earn a seat in the next world." Serving others with a cheerful attitude is deeply cherished.

Over the centuries *seva* has become an essential part of Sikh life. It may take the form of attending to the holy book, sweeping and dusting the shrines, preparing and serving food, or looking after and even cleaning the shoes of worshippers. Young and old, rich and poor, each takes on and performs different tasks. *Seva* also includes serving the community at large by helping to build schools, hospitals, and charity homes. It goes beyond serving fellow Sikhs. It is extended to all, friend and enemy alike.

LANGAR

Langar is both the community meal and the kitchen in which it is prepared. *Langar* is a central part of Sikhism. It testifies to the

ON THE BATTLEFIELD

One Sikh account tells the story of a Sikh soldier named Ghanaya in the army of Guru Gobind Singh. His fellow soldiers saw him giving water to fallen enemies and reported him to the guru. Ghanaya was called in and questioned. He responded that as he moved about the battlefield he had seen neither friend nor foe but only the guru's face. According to this account the guru gave him medicines and bandages and sent him back to help the wounded. Sikhs point to these actions as an example of nonpartisan humanitarian aid to the victims of war that predates the Red Cross and the Red Crescent by centuries.

social equality and familyhood of all people. This fundamental Sikh institution involves the process of preparing meals together as well as eating together. The food used at *langar* is vegetarian so as not to cause offense to anyone. Both men and women engage in preparation and cleanup—chopping vegetables, kneading and rolling out dough, cleaning utensils. Then they sit in a *pangat*, or long row, without regard to caste, race, or religion, and they eat the meal that they have prepared together.

People prepare and fry flat bread for a *langar*, the Sikh community meal, after a worship service. To show equality, at the meal people sit together in long rows rather than at separate tables, and all begin eating at the same time.

COMMUNITY AND EQUALITY

A Sikh bows in prayer on the marble floor in the precincts of the Harimandir, the Golden Temple in Amritsar. Hundreds of thousands of Sikhs visit the Golden Temple annually and a *langar* is open to all visitors and pilgrims. The three institutions fostered by Guru Nanak—*seva, langar,* and *sangat*—have remained important social and religious structures for the Sikhs. Through them Guru Nanak's followers formed a tightly knit community that has evolved into a distinct Sikh identity.

In Nanak's time the idea of different castes eating together was bold and revolutionary. Yet Nanak understood the importance of a shared meal in creating a feeling of belonging and fellowship. Like the Thanksgiving feast or the Christmas dinner, like the Jewish seder or the other traditional meals, all of which are shared by people who are close or part of a community, *langar* creates a feeling of family. It extends the concept of the family meal as a step toward bonding human beings regardless of race, gender, caste, and class.

The *langar* as an instrument of social change continued to gain importance under the leadership of the successive gurus. In Guru Angad's day his wife, Mata Khivi, was known for the rich and delicious meals she served. The third guru, Amar Das, insisted that visitors first enjoy *langar* with the community before meeting with him. "First *pangat*, then meeting with the guru," he decreed.

Some Sikhs consider *langar* to be a way of earning merit toward rebirth and their next life. In modern times the custom is still very much in evidence in India, not only in the *gurdwaras* but beyond. During certain celebrations, such as the birthday of a guru, the celebration of an important historical event, or the martyrdom of a Sikh hero, *langar* is everywhere, even on the highways and byways. Sikhs of all ages arrange themselves in rows to block the road or they lay tree trunks across it to stop the flow of traffic. They stop the speeding buses, cars, and trucks, the slow-going bullock carts, rickshaws, and pedestrians, and they enthusiastically serve *langar* to the drivers and passengers.

SANGAT

Sangat is the Sikh gathering, or local community. Sikhs prize comradeship and company with others, and the fellowship of the *sangat* is of primary importance in their religious practice. The tradition of an active and fruitful involvement with the community comes from Nanak himself, and Sikhs see community participation as an essential part of their faith. According to a popular Sikh saying, "One disciple is a single Sikh, two form a holy association, but where there are five present, there is the Ultimate Reality Itself."

Like *langar, sangat* is open to all. Members of Sikh congregations sit on the floor singing hymns, listening to readings from the holy text, reciting verses, and praying. The inclusive nature of *sangat* dates to the time of Nanak, who welcomed everyone who wished to follow him. The historian Bhai Gurdas notes that wherever Nanak went *sangat* soon emerged. Bhai Gurdas describes the daily schedule at Kartarpur, with the community gathering for evening hymns and morning prayers: "In the evening *arti* and *sohila* were sung and in the morning was recited the Jap (a hymn)."

Treasure of the Divine Name

Sangat is a mode of both spiritual and moral inspiration. According to Nanak: "Through *sangat*, one obtains the treasure of the Divine Nam. . . . Just as iron rubbed against the philosopher's stone turns into gold, so does dark ignorance transform into brilliant light in company of the good." Participation with others becomes a force for inspiring the spiritual quest.

THE TRADITION OF THE GURUS

At the end of his life Nanak established yet another tradition of far-reaching importance for the Sikhs. He called one of his faithful disciples, Lehna, to him and gave him the name Angad, which literally means "a part of his own self." Nanak placed five copper coins and a coconut before Lehna and bowed down at his feet. Thus Lehna became Guru Angad, the second guru in Sikh history and the new leader of the Sikh community.

Sikhs believe that by naming him Angad, Nanak had made Lehna more than his successor. He had transferred his own inner light to Lehna, making Lehna one with him in spirit. The Sikh scripture describes the transference as being like one flame kindling another. The light and the message had passed from Nanak to Angad. This transference, begun by Nanak, was repeated successively through the installation of the 10th guru, Gobind Singh, in 1675.

THE 10 GURUS OF SIKHISM

The 10 gurus of the Sikh tradition are unique in the history of religion. The same light is reflected in ten different bodies, and the same voice speaks through all 10. However, the guru in Sikhism does not represent the Ultimate Reality in any way. The guru is not divine nor is he a Christlike figure. The guru is a channel, a guide who enlightens people and enables them to understand the love and nature of the Divine Reality.

The 10 Gurus of Sikhism
(1469–1539) **Guru Nanak**
(1504–52 became guru 1539) **Guru Angad**
(1479–74 became guru 1552) **Guru Amar Das**
(1534–81 became guru 1574) **Guru Ram Das**
(1563–1606 became guru 1581) **Guru Arjan**
(1595–1644 became guru 1606) **Guru Hargobind**
(1630–61 became guru 1644) **Guru Har Rai**
(1656–64 became guru 1661) **Guru Har Krishan**
(1621–75 became guru 1664) **Guru Tegh Bahadur**
(1666–1708 became guru 1675) **Guru Gobind Singh**

THE ELEVENTH AND FINAL GURU

The 10th guru, Gobind Singh, ended the line of personal gurus by passing the succession not to another person but to the Guru Granth, the holy book of the Sikhs. From that time on the light and voice of the Ultimate Reality have been transmitted by the scriptures. Thus the message and the mission begun by Guru Nanak continued through nine more gurus and reached culmination in the Guru Granth.

GURU NANAK'S DEATH

Nanak died on September 7, 1539. The *Janamsakhi* story records that after Nanak's death his sheet-covered body was claimed by both Hindus and Muslims, each group wanting to perform the last rites. According to their customs the Hindus wanted to cremate Nanak's body; the Muslims, to bury it. However when the sheet was pulled away, nothing was there but flowers. According to the story the sheet and the flowers were divided between the Muslims and the Hindus to be disposed of according to the beliefs of each group. The body of Nanak had vanished, leaving behind the message of universal harmony for generations to come.

CHAPTER 3

SIKH TRADITION AND THE GURU GRANTH

The Guru Granth, the holy book of the Sikhs, is 1,430 pages long and is written entirely in verse. It is the longest book of rhymed poetry in the world. The word *granth* simply means "book," and *guru* signifies that this particular *granth* has been designated the "guru," or giver of enlightenment for all Sikhs. The Guru Granth is the focal point of all Sikh rituals and ceremonies. Wherever it rests, that space becomes holy.

THE COMPILING OF THE GURU GRANTH

After Nanak's divine revelation at the River Bein he sang a song of joy. Throughout his ministry, inspired by the Divine One, he sang and recited many more verses. The sacred songs of Nanak were the beginning of Sikh scripture.

Nanak's poems express a range of experience from great joy to deep grief. They tell of his longing to be united with the Infinite Divine One, his awe at the grandeur and vastness of creation, and his sympathy for fellow beings in bondage and oppression. Sikhs believe that Nanak's poetry was not consciously created but

A Sikh man reads from the Guru Granth, the Sikh holy book, during a wedding service in the *gurdwara*. The Granth is written in Gurmukhi, a script devised specifically for the purpose of recording the gurus' words. *Gurmukhi* means "from the guru's mouth."

When Angad inherited the guru-ship from Nanak and became the second guru, or teacher, of Sikhism, he continued the tradition of sacred poetry, which he felt was important for the beauty it brought to human life as well as for the knowledge it transmitted. "It is ambrosia (heavenly nectar), it is the essence of all, it emerges from deep knowledge and intense concentration," Angad wrote. To record the sacred word Angad developed a written form of the Punjabi language, Gurmukhi script. He added his own poetry to that of Nanak and signed it with his pseudonym—Nanak.

sprang spontaneously from his lips. As he spoke his followers copied down the holy words. All believed his words to be divinely inspired: "To you belong my breath, to you my flesh," says the poet Nanak, "you the True One are my Beloved." The Sikh historian Bhai Gurdas says that Nanak carried a manuscript of his poems with him. The *Janamsakhi* records that before his death Nanak passed his Word, recorded in written form, to his successor, Angad.

PASSING ON THE TRADITION

As the guruship passed successively from one guru to the next, so did each guru's words. Each guru valued and preserved the literary inheritance from those before him and thus each passed the body of poetry to the next after adding his own poetry. Each guru signed his composition with the name Nanak. In that way each affirmed his unity with Nanak, who continued to speak through all of them. The third guru, Amar Das, not only added his own poetic compositions and songs but also included those of some of the Hindu and Muslim saints. The two volumes he collected survive to this day.

BUILDING A COMMON MESSAGE

By 1603 Sikhism was no longer contained in one small area. It had spread geographically and grown in its numbers. During a famine in the Punjab Guru Arjan had traveled widely from village to village, helping to sink wells and performing other kinds of public service. As a result many people had joined the Sikh *panth*. They needed a common message for their spiritual and moral life, a text that would give a single, definite form to Sikh beliefs. And then there was the problem of counterfeit works. The Adi Granth (which means "First Book") was supposed to record the words of Nanak and the gurus who had directly succeeded him, but the succession was not completely free of problems. Ram Das, the fourth guru, had bypassed his older sons and appointed his younger son, Arjan, to the guruship. However Pirthi Chand, Arjan's eldest brother, and Pirthi's son Meharban were composing sacred poetry and signing it with the name Nanak. Arjan feared that the words of his predecessors would become diluted.

COLLATING THE HYMNS

Arjan, the fifth guru, undertook the job of compiling an authorized version of the holy Adi Granth. He began to draw the Sikh literary legacy into an authorized volume for coming generations. The task was a difficult one. Arjan called on the historian Bhai

---

CONTRIBUTORS TO THE GURU GRANTH

The Sikh Gurus
(1469–1539) **Guru Nanak:** 974 hymns
(1439–1552) **Guru Angad:** 62 couplets
(1552–74) **Guru Amar Das:** 907 hymns
(1574–81) **Guru Ram Das:** 638 hymns
(1581–1606) **Guru Arjan:** 2,218 hymns
(1664–75) **Guru Tegh Bahadur:** 59 hymns and 56 couplets
    (added by **Guru Gobind Singh** (1675–1708)

Hindu Bhaktas

Kabir: 292 hymns and 243 couplets
Farid: 4 hymns and 130 couplets
Namdev: 60 hymns
Ravidas: 41 hymns
Jaidev: 2 hymns
Beni: 3 hymns
Trilochan: 4 hymns
Parmananda: 1 hymn
Sadhana: 1 hymn
Ramananda: 1 hymn

Islamic Sufis

Dhanna: 4 hymns
Pipa: 1 hymn
Sain: 1 hymn
Bhikhan: 2 hymns
Sur Das: 2 hymns
Sundar: 1 hymn
Mardana: 3 couplets
Satta and Balvand: 1 hymn
Bhatts: 123 *swaiyyas* (quatrains)

A *granthi* reading the Guru Granth Sahib in a *gurdwara* in Amritsar.

Gurdas for help. They chose a serene and picturesque spot in a forest outside the town of Amritsar in which to work. Today this site is marked by a shrine called Ramsar. By now a vast amount of poetry had been handed down. Arjan himself had composed thousands of hymns. Selections had to be made from his poems as well as from the works of the preceding four gurus. In addition Arjan wanted to represent Hindu and Muslim saints whose works were in harmony with Sikh belief. Finally what was genuine had to be sifted from what was not. As they worked Bhai Gurdas copied the chosen pieces in Gurmukhi script, a script devised specifically for the purpose of recording the gurus' words. *Gurmukhi* means "from the guru's mouth."

ORGANIZING THE POEMS

Arjan arranged the selected compositions according to their musical patterns. Except for a few poems that he left to stand alone, Arjan organized the collection into 31 sections. Each section contains poems written in one raga, or melody pattern—a form in Hindu music having the melodic rhythm prescribed by tradition. The seven ragas appear in a particular order. Each raga has its own distinctive intervals, rhythms, and timing, and each is associated with a particular season of the year.

Within each of the 31 sections of the Adi Granth Arjan arranged the compositions in a particular order. First came the works of the earlier gurus in the order of their succession. Since all of the gurus had signed their poems Nanak, Arjan distinguished them by using the word *Mahalla*, which means "body," and a number. Thus poems headed *Mahalla 1* were the work of the first guru, those headed *Mahalla 2* were the work of the second guru, and so on. This designation symbolized the belief that each guru shared the spirit of Nanak in his body. After the gurus' poems Arjan placed the works of a number of Hindu saints and one Muslim, Sheikh Farid, as well as others born before Guru Nanak such as Bhai Kabir who, as a poet and religious reformer, drew together aspects of the Hindu Bhakti movement and Islamic Sufism.

A SACRED TEXT IN A SACRED PLACE

The completion of the Adi Granth was an occasion for great celebration. On August 16, 1604, Sikhs traveled far to witness the colorful procession that would bear the sacred volume to Harimandir, the temple at Amritsar. Harimandir, a special place for Sikh worship, was the inspiration of Amar Das, the third guru.

Yearning for the Divine

The first of the seven ragas, or melody patterns, is Sri, which means "supreme." It is a basic melody pattern from which others are derived. The Sikhs compare Sri to the philosopher's stone, an imaginary substance that ancient people believed could transform base metals such as iron into gold. Sri is sung in the evening, the time of advancing darkness. In content too it expresses the darkness of ignorance and superstition in society before Nanak's ministry. Sri is also associated with extreme heat and cold or extremes of emotion. The hymns in the Sri pattern express a great yearning for the Divine.

Looking across the reflecting pool to the Harimandir, the Golden Temple at Amritsar. Work on Harimandir had begun under Ram Das, the fourth guru, in 1577. A structure of great architectural beauty that drew on both Hindu and Muslim design, the temple had been completed in 1601, only three years before the completion of the Guru Granth. Harimandir came to be known as the Golden Temple after the Sikh maharaja Ranjit Singh had it reconstructed and plated with gold.

The Adi Granth was carried on the head of an elderly and much respected Sikh follower, Bhai Buddha, who was the first priest, known as a *granthi*. The name Buddha had come to mean "very wise and old." Bhai Buddha was both and was often consulted on very important matters. For example the decision to appoint Guru Arjan to become the fifth guru was based on his advice.

Arjan walked behind him holding a whisk over the holy book to shade and protect it from flies, other insects, and dust. Musicians played hymns from its pages. Observers likened the atmosphere to that of a joyous wedding.

Once inside Bhai Buddha reverently opened the Adi Granth to obtain the *hukm*, or Divine Command, while Arjan stood in attendance. At dusk the Adi Granth was taken to a special chamber and placed on a pedestal. Arjan remained with it, sleeping on the floor by its side to show the esteem in which he held it.

Thus during Arjan's time the Sikhs acquired both a sacred space in which to worship and a sacred text to guide them. Both helped to mold the Sikhs' consciousness of themselves and their faith. The Golden Temple at Amritsar provided a central place for gathering and worship. When the last human guru, Guru Gobind Singh, made the Adi Granth the final guru, the title of the book changed to the Guru Granth Sahib, though it is also still called the Adi Granth. The Guru Granth gave the Sikh message concrete form. The holy book not only became a spiritual and religious guide, but it also shaped the intellectual and cultural environment.

THE RISE OF SIKH MILITARISM

The Punjab at this time was ruled by the Muslim Mughal dynasty. During the lifetime of the third, fourth, and fifth gurus the Mughal emperor was the remarkable Akbar (1556–1605). He showed great interest in all religions and, although a Muslim, often engaged in discussion with leaders of different religions. He was a friend of Guru Arjan and spoke of the Adi Granth with great praise, despite the fact that some of his Muslim advisers claimed it insulted Muslim teachings. However his son Jahangir was a very different kind of man and in 1606, within a year of coming to power, he had Guru Arjan arrested, tortured, and killed. Throughout the trials he faced Guru Arjan spoke words of peace and conciliation. The Sikhs viewed Arjan as a martyr to the faith and his death generated a strong impulse for self-defense.

SWORDS OF *PIRI* AND *MIRI*

Arjan's son, Hargobind, succeeded him as guru. On the day that he was to be invested Hargobind appeared dressed as a warrior. He put on two swords. The sword of *piri* symbolized the spiritual power of guruship; the sword of *miri* symbolized earthly power. Together the swords represented the joining of the heavenly and earthly aspects of Sikhism. With that action a new era began. The meekness and gentleness that had characterized the Sikh population was replaced by armed resistance.

Hargobind raised an armed band of Sikhs and let it be known that future disciples were to come bearing gifts of horses and weapons. In 1609 he built a fortress called the Iron Fort to defend the town of Amritsar. In front of the Golden Temple he built the Akal Takht, or "Throne of the Formless One." Harimandir, the Golden Temple, was for prayer alone. Secular affairs would be conducted from the Akal Takht. This martial atmosphere intensified after the death of Tegh Bahadur, the ninth guru.

SAVIOR OF HINDUS

Tegh Bahadur had come to the defense of the Hindu population, whom the Muslim rulers were forcing to convert to Islam. Hindu Brahmins came from Kashmir (a region in today's northern India and northeastern Pakistan) to ask Guru Tegh Bahadur to help defend the Hindu communities, and when he and the Sikhs assisted them the guru became known as the Savior of the Hindus. For his stand on religious freedom Tegh Bahadur was imprisoned and beheaded in 1675 under the order of the Muslim emperor. Tegh Bahadur's son, Gobind Singh, was only nine years old at the time. Nevertheless he became the 10th guru and carried on the moral and spiritual legacy with great fervor.

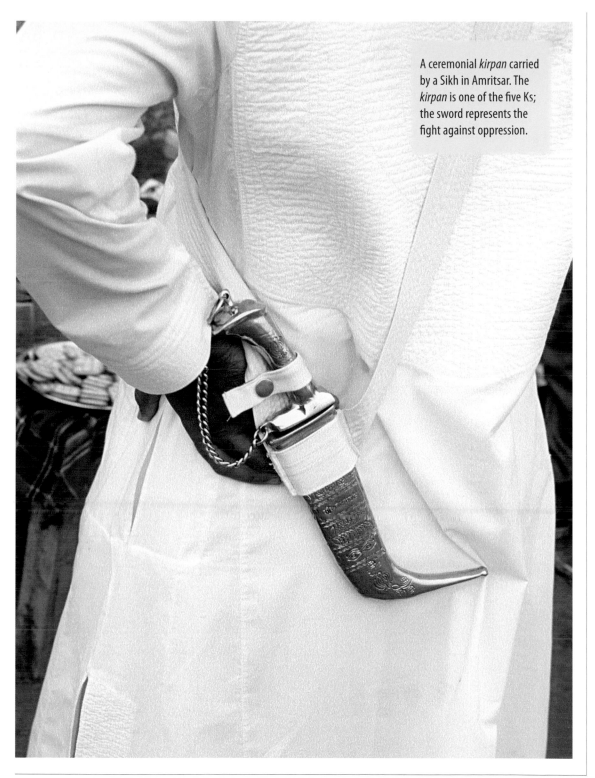

A ceremonial *kirpan* carried by a Sikh in Amritsar. The *kirpan* is one of the five Ks; the sword represents the fight against oppression.

On March 30, 1699, on Baisakhi, a traditional Hindu festival date, Guru Gobind Singh called his people together at Anandpur, a town in the Shivalik hills (part of the Himalayas). According to the accounts of contemporary Sikh historians and Muslim writers large numbers of Sikhs arrived for the festival and an air of anticipation ran through the crowd. At last Gobind Singh appeared dressed in full battle gear and carrying a gleaming sword. The guru reminded the people of the need for unity and courage against persecution. Then holding up his weapon he cried, "My sword today wants a head. Let any one of my true Sikhs come forward."

Gobind Singh's singular demand numbed the assembly. For a long moment no one moved, no one uttered a word. Gobind Singh repeated his words. People were stunned. They could not believe their ears. The guru wanted one of them to volunteer to die! Confusion turned to fear and a murmur of dismay ran through the gathered crowd. The guru repeated the call. This time a man stood up. His name was Daya Ram and he was a Hindu farmer from Lahore. He walked forward and Gobind Singh escorted him into a nearby tent.

The crowd waited—but not for long. Gobind Singh emerged from the tent, his sword dripping with blood. To the horror of the onlookers he called for another head. This was more than the people could endure. Many began to leave. Some asked the guru's mother to stop him. However another man, Dharam Das, stood up to offer himself to the guru's sword.

PANJ PYARE—THE FIVE BELOVED

Dharam Das was escorted into the tent and again the guru returned with a bloodied sword. Now he demanded a third head. Five times in all Gobind Singh led a man into the tent, and four times he returned to the horrified crowd with his sword dripping blood. The people had seen Mokham Chand, Himmat, and Sahib Chand follow the first two men into the tent. When would it end? Then the guru reappeared with all five men, now dressed like the guru himself in military garb and wearing swords of their own. The guru thus introduced the courageous *Panj Pyare,* or "Five Beloved," who had been willing to follow their guru even to death, ready to stand up for justice and freedom.

THE KHALSA

These five men became the first members of the Khalsa—the "Pure Ones." By their willingness to die for their faith they were reborn into a new order, a brotherhood with the guru himself. Membership in this new order severed all previous family ties and each member received a new surname: Singh, meaning "lion." No longer would these men be bound by the restrictions of their castes, hereditary occupations, or earlier rituals. They swore to fight fearlessly and to give their lives willingly for their faith, to have faith in the One, and to consider all human beings equal, without regard to caste or religion.

The guru poured water into a steel bowl and stirred it with his sword, chanting verses from the Adi Granth. His wife, who became known as the mother of the Khalsa nation, dropped some sugar into the bowl and its sweetness mingled with the touch of steel, creating *amrita,* the nectar used in the Sikh baptismal ritual. The five then drank from the same bowl—something they could not have done when bound by the traditions of the Hindu caste system—and thus sealed their pledge of equality and faithfulness.

ONE CREED AND ONE PATH

Guru Gobind Singh, the tenth guru, spoke the following words to the new members of the Khalsa, the "Pure Ones" who were willing to follow their guru even to death:

I wish you all to embrace one creed and follow one path, rising above all differences of religion as now practiced. Let the four Hindu castes, who

Guru Eternal

The Adi Granth became the Guru Granth, the Guru Eternal of the Sikh people, and the line of gurus that had begun with Nanak came to an end. From that day on Sikhs have revered the Guru Granth as both the Divine Word and the physical representation of their guru. In their daily prayers, morning and evening, Sikhs recite: "Acknowledge the Guru Granth as the visible body of the Gurus."

Young boys dressed in their Khalsa clothes during a procession in the Punjab to remember the Martyrdom of Guru Tegh Bahadur. Some of their turbans are pinned with the *khanda* symbol, at the center is a double-edged sword representing the creative power of God, surrounded by a circle representing the unity of God. The outer swords, crossed at the bottom, represent *piri* and *miri,* the spiritual and temporal power of God.

have different duties laid down for them in their scriptures, abandon them altogether, and adopting the way of mutual help and cooperation, mix freely with one another. Do not follow the old scriptures. Let none pay homage to the Ganges and other places of pilgrimage which are considered to be holy in the Hindu religion, or worship the Hindu deities such as Rama, Krishna, Brahma, and Durga, and so forth, but all should cherish faith in the teachings of Guru Nanak and his successors. Let each of the four castes receive my Baptism of the double-edged sword, eat out of the same vessel, and feel no aloofness from, or contempt for, one another.

(In Kapur Singh, *The Baisakhi of Guru Gobind Singh;* a quote from Sujan Rai Bhandari Batalia in *Khulasat-ut-Tawarikh.*)

LION AND PRINCESS

In creating the Khalsa Gobind Singh gave practical form to Nanak's vision of the Oneness of Ultimate Reality and the Oneness of all people. He called on the faithful to "recognize the singular caste of humanity," words that are still recited by Sikhs everywhere. He made the *amrita* ceremony, or baptism, available to both men and women and invited the women to wear the symbols of the Khalsa too. As men would receive the surname Singh, meaning "lion," women would receive the surname Kaur, meaning "princess," which they would retain even after they married. Gobind Singh's declaration thus changed the patriarchal structure of Sikh society. From that time on men and women no longer traced their ancestry to their fathers. As Singh and Kaur both became equal partners in the new family of Sikhism.

THE GRANTH IS NAMED GURU

Contemporary Sikh historians record the passing of the holy authority of guru from Gobind Singh to the Adi Granth. According to their accounts on October 6, 1708, Guru Gobind Singh lay dying. He had not yet named a successor and his disciples wondered on whom the mantle of guruship would fall. At last the guru called for the Adi Granth. When his disciples brought the holy book to him Gobind Singh placed a coin and a coconut before it, much as Nanak had done in naming Angad Guru as his sucessor. Gobind Singh bowed his head in reverence. Then he commanded the gathered community to acknowledge the Adi Granth as the guru in his place. The Adi Granth became the final Guru, the Guru Granth Sahib.

THE CONTENTS OF THE GURU GRANTH

The Guru Granth opens with the number One. It is the first word of the first statement of Guru Nanak: *Ikk oan kar*—literally, "One Reality Is," or "There is one Being." All 1,430 pages of the Guru Granth expand on these three words.

These first three words are the fundamental affirmation of Sikhism. The Guru Granth then describes the Reality, its relation to the world, and its relation to the people of the world. Overall the Guru Granth contains no historical narratives and no biographical details as do the Jewish and Christian Bibles. The Sikh holy book is composed of spiritually exalted poetry. Its core theme is the individual's longing for the Ultimate Reality, while other sections give guidance for daily living—for example not eating halal meat (meat of an animal killed by ritual slaughter) and always engaging in an honorable trade.

IKK OAN KAR

Ikk oan kar is both a verbal and a visual statement. Like the Christian cross it serves as a central symbol depicted on gateways, walls, medallions, canopies, fabric, and even jewelry.

Ikk, the concept of Oneness, was central to Nanak's vision and to his message. His society was torn by religious conflict that ran counter to the oneness of the Ultimate Reality that Nanak preached. He understood the Ultimate Reality as being without form or image and not confined to space, time, or gender. What human term would describe it? In which language? Instead of writing the word *ikk* or coining a new word to express oneness, Nanak used the number One to express the Ultimate Reality. The number One transcended barriers of language, could be understood by people of all cultures, was visible to all, simple and universal.

The second word, *oan,* or "Reality," is the same as the Sanskrit *om.* The symbol for the third word, *kar,* or "Is," is an unending arch that symbolizes the eternal nature of the One that is without beginning or end.

Mundavani—the Seal

The Guru Granth ends with the *mundavani,* the seal, or final word, of its compiler, the fifth guru, Arjan:

*On the platter lie arranged
three delicacies:
Truth, contentment, and
contemplation …
All who eat them, all who savor them
Obtain liberation.*

THE "THREE DELICACIES"

The Guru Granth invites the Sikhs to partake of its offerings, its "three delicacies" of truth, contentment, and contemplation. Through them followers may understand the fundamental essence of the universe, satisfy spiritual hunger, and anchor the restless mind and spirit in contemplation.

Intellectual understanding is not enough for complete fulfillment, however. The offerings are also to be savored and enjoyed. The poetry of the Guru Granth

calls for an aesthetic experience, a total emotional and mental response from the reader.

THE GURU GRANTH IN SIKH LIFE

The Guru Granth is the continuing spiritual and historical authority for the Sikhs as well as the source of their literary inspiration. The community's ideals, institutions, and rituals derive their meaning from it. Ceremonies related to birth, initiation, marriage, and death take place in its presence. Harbans Singh,

Sikh symbols on the Guru Granth Sahib in a *gurdwara*. The *Ikk oan kar* symbol—There Is Only One God—is on the left at the back, engraved on the shield, and in the foreground. Two *khanda* symbols, represented by swords, are at the back, in the middle and on the right.

an eminent Sikh scholar, asserts that the physical presence of the Guru Granth and its poetic contents are the two main forces that have shaped the Sikhs' conduct and their sense of what it means to be Sikh.

Every day in Sikh homes and in *gurdwaras* Sikhs open the Guru Granth at dawn. This act of opening the holy book is called *prakash*, "making the light manifest." Any baptized Sikh may perform *prakash*; in Sikh homes the duty often rotates among family members, and in *gurdwaras* among *sangat* members. The book is draped in a rich silk and brocade cloth called *rumala*, placed on quilted mats, and supported by

Members of a Sikh community in New York singing *kirtan*, Sikh sacred hymns, in the shrine room of a *gurdwara*.

three cushions, one under each side and one in the center. A canopy hangs over it for protection and a whisk waves over it as a sign of respect. Those present stand humbly in front of it and recite Ardas, a prayer of supplication. The Guru Granth is then opened at random and the passage at the top of the left-hand page is read aloud. This passage is called *vak,* the order or message for the day.

After dusk the Guru Granth is closed. The closing ritual is called *sukhasan,* which means "to sit comfortably." Again Ardas is said and *vak* taken. Evening prayers known as Rahiras are recited and the Guru Granth is closed.

Special Readings

In times of uncertainty and difficulty or in times of celebration and hope, the Guru Granth is read through from beginning to end. The reading may be *saptoh,* a seven-day reading, or it may be *akhand,* a 48-hour nonstop reading of the Guru Granth, during which several readers, called *granthis,* take turns reading. There are other special readings as well. In *sampa,* one particular hymn is repeated after each passage. A *khulla* reading is one that Sikhs undertake privately, and it may take a month or a year to complete.

CHAPTER 4

SIKH THOUGHT

The Guru Granth begins with a short passage called the Mul Mantra. The few lines in this passage state the essential creed, the basic belief, of the Sikh religion. The Mul Mantra precedes the Jap—the first hymn composed by Guru Nanak—and devout Sikhs recite the 38 stanzas of the Jap every morning. In a shortened version the Mul Mantra can also be found introducing many different sections of the Guru Granth. The Mul Mantra is at the heart of Sikh thought.

Like other mantras the Mul Mantra is a portion of a prayer of special beauty and power. It is rhythmic and brief. Great meaning is packed into its few words. In the original Punjabi it is not written in sentences but in a few individual words and images that together express the fundamental focus of Sikhism. In these words and images the Mul Mantra expresses Sikh metaphysics—

Preparing to read from the Guru Granth, a Sikh waves a *chouri,* or whisk, in homage over the holy scriptures. Anyone, male or female, who can read Gurmukhi script may read the Guru Granth anywhere, either in a *gurdwara* or in a private home. Usually when a family owns a copy of the Guru Granth, the book occupies a special room. Sikhs respect the poetry of the Hindu and Muslim saints in the Guru Granth as much as they do the poetry of their gurus. Thus, in their daily practice, the Sikhs continue to live according to Guru Nanak's words: "There is no Hindu; there is no Muslim."

Because the Mul Mantra, the short passage found at the beginning of the Guru Granth is difficult to translate, many different versions exist. Here is one version:

Ikk oan kar	There is one Being
sat nam	Truth is its name
karta purakh	Creator of all
nir bhau	Without fear
nir vair	Without enmity
akal murat	Timeless in form
ajuni	Unborn
saibhang	Self-existent
gur prasad	[Discovered] through the gift of the enlightener

the belief in the nature of being and reality and the relationship of individuals to the universe.

Sikhism's most fundamental belief is expressed in the first three words of the Mul Mantra: *Ikk oan kar,* "There is one Being."

IKK

The first word of the Mul Mantra is usually written as the number One and proclaims the existence and total Oneness of the Ultimate Reality. In the Mul Mantra this Ultimate Reality is defined by what it is not: It is without human form and is genderless. It is not limited by space or time. It has no color and no shape, no beginning and no end. It fears nothing and is at odds with nothing. With these words Sikhism rejects outright the Hindu belief in *avtarvad,* or divine incarnation, the embodiment of a god in human form. Moreover, because the Ultimate Reality has no form it cannot be represented visually. There can be no pictures or statues of it. In fact there is no way to portray it at all.

REACHING THE ONE

Yet Sikh scripture wholeheartedly accepts and affirms the many ways of reaching the Singular Reality, or the One. Nanak never asked people to renounce their religions. On the contrary he asked them to acknowledge and be whoever they were as fully as possible. Of the Hindus he asked that they be authentic Hindus; of the Muslims that they be authentic Muslims. The One is common to people from all faiths and cultures.

Arjan, the fifth guru, reinforced Nanak's vision. He declared that underneath, all true religions are the same: "Some call it Rama, some call it Khuda ; some worship it as Vishnu; some as Allah." By stressing the basic similarity of the Hindu and Islamic traditions, represented respectively by Rama (a Hindu deity) and Khuda (the Islamic name of God in Urdu, the language widely used by Muslims), Sikh gurus tried to bring peace and harmony to their divided society. To Sikhs the differences were superficial—formalities and externals only.

WITHOUT IMAGE OR FORM

This Oneness of Reality forms the bedrock of Sikhism. As a result scholars categorize Sikhism as a monotheistic religion. Yet to term Sikhism mono-*theistic* misses an important part of Guru Nanak's vision. Sikhism does not subscribe to a belief in a majestic Theos, or personal god. The Sikh Reality is indeed One, but it has no image or form. For Nanak the One is the experience of utter infinity: *Ikk oan kar.* This dimension of personal experience is central to Sikh thought.

OAN

From the rich variety of Arabic, Persian, and Sanskrit words that he might have used to express the One, Nanak chose the Punjabi word *oan.* The Sanskrit word for the same concept, *aum* or *om,* means "existence."

The Mandukya Upanishad, a Hindu scripture, explains *aum* as a four-level journey of the mind. The first stage, *A,* is the realm of consciousness. In that stage people are aware of the world and of their separateness from others: *I* versus *it* or *them.* The second stage, *U,* is the subcon-

The Ultimate Reality

The Ultimate Reality is the same for all people. In the words of Guru Gobind Singh found in the Guru Granth:

. . . Hindus and Muslims are one!
The same Reality is the creator and preserver of all;
Know no distinctions between them.
The monastery and the mosque are the same;
So are the Hindu form of worship (puja) and the Muslim prayer (namaz).
Humans are all one!

The Symbol of Sikhism

The symbol of Sikhism, which stands for bravery and spiritual power and which flies over *gurdwaras* everywhere, consists of two curved swords to remind Sikhs to serve the Ultimate Reality by teaching the truth and by fighting to defend what is right; a discus, or circle, to serve as a reminder to all Sikhs that Reality is one; and in the middle a *khanda,* the double-edged sword used to prepare *amrita,* or nectar of immortality.

scious state in which absolute categories start to break down. In that state people experience an expansion of the mind. The logical world begins to dissolve and, transported by a higher consciousness, one might experience being in two places at the same time. The third stage, M, is a state of deep sleep, or total unconsciousness. It is like sleeping so soundly that one does not recall the difference between having slept for a minute or for an entire day.

In the fourth and final stage the A, the U, and the M are fused. This is the experience of total unity. In this state the self experiences a state of oneness with the Ultimate Reality. For the Sikhs Guru Nanak's use of *Oan,* or *Aum,* expresses the belief that the Ultimate Reality is an inner experience rather than an objective knowledge of God.

SAT NAM

The second line of the Mul Mantra, *sat nam,* literally means "Truth is the Name." The first stanza of the Guru Granth's first hymn, the Jap, explains further: "Truth it has been from timeless eternity. Truth it has been within circles of temporality. Truth it is in the present, and Truth it shall be forever."

To the Sikhs Truth is not an objective category but a way of being. Immediately after the statement on Truth the Jap asks, "How to live a Truthful life? How to break the barriers of falsity?" The transition from Truth to true living is immediate and spontaneous. Reality is not just known objectively. It must be lived.

OTHER SIKH PHILOSOPHY

In its first two lines the Mul Mantra introduces the fundamental beliefs of Sikhism. Other ideas, central to Sikh philosophy and thought, but not directly stated, in the Mul Mantra, follow logically from it.

The Fearless, Formless One

In focusing on the One Sikhism rejects the many gods of Hinduism. Guru Nanak states, "In comparison with the Fearless, Formless One, innumerable gods are as dust." The One is above the traditional Hindu deities such as Vishnu the Preserver and Siva the Destroyer. "Millions of Vishnus has It created, millions of universes has It spawned, millions of Sivas has It raised and assimilated," says the Guru Granth.

Natural cycles such as growth and death are also maintained through *hukm,* an Arabic word meaning "Divine Order" or "Divine Will." So is the psychological and physical makeup of human beings. Their feelings and emotions, such actions as seeing, talking, hearing, or walking, and their blessings and misfortunes all come from the Divine Will. In the Guru Granth *hukm* is presented as the all-embracing principle that governs all activity. *Hukm* is not apart from the world. It is a link between the universe and its divine Source and Preserver.

NADAR

Nadar is a Persian word loosely translated as "grace." It is related to the Persian *nazar,* meaning "sight" or "vision." In Sikh thought *nadar* refers to the divine glance of favor. Everyone and everything exist within the orbit of divine vision: "All action takes place within its sight; nothing happens outside of it." The unsleeping eye of *nadar* on the world is a sign of the benevolent aspect of the Ultimate One. *Nadar* is esteemed as a precious gift.

DEATH AND REBIRTH

In general Sikhs believe that after they die they will be reborn into the world in a new form. Their good deeds in this life can help them to achieve a better future life. However *nadar,* the benevolent glance, can break the cycle of death and rebirth. Instead of being born into a new body a person can be united with the Formless One. According to the Jap, "Through actions one achieves the body, but, through the benevolent glance (*nadar*), one attains liberation from the cycle of birth and death." *Nadar* thus allows Sikhs to reach their ideal, a state of not simply knowing the Ultimate Reality, but of being one with it.

Hukm—Divine Will

Hukm is an Arabic word meaning "Divine Order" or "Divine Will." As Creator of All, the Ultimate Reality operates through it. Both creation and continuing life depend on *hukm.* The beginning of the world is the outcome of *hukm.* Sikh philosophy claims that the genesis of the world cannot be known: "No one knows the time nor the hour, nor the date, nor the month, nor the season when creation originated . . . Through *hukm* everything came to be but what the *hukm* is, no one can describe," says Nanak in the Jap. In accordance with *hukm,* the Divine Will, all of creation sprang forth in its countless varieties.

Sikh pilgrims passing through a gateway leading to the Harimandir
(House of God), the Golden Temple in Amritsar, the holiest of Sikh shrines.
The temple rests on a platform in the middle of a sacred reflecting pool.

SABAD—"WORD"

Sabad is translated as "Word." In Sikh thought *sabad* is both the way in which the Divine is revealed and the path leading to the Divine Reality. The Guru Granth says that "The singular One has neither form nor color nor any material; but It is manifested through the true Word (*sabad*)." Like reality the Word has no substance. It cannot be seen or touched. So it is appropriate that the Word represent the formless nature of the Ultimate, which is transcendent, above all things in the physical universe.

It was through the Divine Word that Nanak's revelation at the River Bein came. He saw no Being but he clearly heard the call. According to Sikh belief everyone is endowed with an inner voice that speaks a Divine message. This is the *anahad sabad,* the "Soundless Word." How may the Soundless Word be heard? How may people learn to recognize the Divine within? The answer again is *sabad*. The so-called Word of the gurus clears the way so that individuals can hear the Word within themselves.

THE TRUTH IN EACH INDIVIDUAL

The final line of the Mul Mantra, *gur prasad,* states that *ikk oan kar,* the One, is recognized through the "gift of the enlightener"— that is, through the grace of the guru. Again this knowledge is not purely intellectual. Rather it is a deeply felt truth that echoes within each person. The gurus do not present an external truth. Instead the Word evokes a harmonic response from a Truth that is already inside every individual.

PHYSICAL IMAGES

In the Guru Granth the gurus endeavor to express the abstract concepts of Sikh philosophy in concrete images. They describe the special relationship between the Ultimate Reality and humankind in terms of intimate human relationships. "You are my father, you are my mother, you are my brother, you are my friend," says Guru Arjan.

Images of conception, the growth of the unborn child in its mother's womb, and birth express the creative force of the Ulti-

The Unfathomable Beloved

Marriage, the highest experience of human love, becomes a metaphor that describes the longing for the Ultimate Reality. A bride awaiting her divine groom addresses the Ultimate Reality in intimate terms: "O my handsome, unfathomable Beloved," she says. In another verse she lavishly praises the One: "My groom is utterly glorious, brilliantly crimson, compassionate, beneficent, beloved, enticer of the hearts, overflowing with beauty like the crimson flower."

mate. "From mother's blood and father's semen is created the human form," says the Guru Granth. "In the warmth of mother's womb are we first formed."

The writers often speak from the point of view of a woman who addresses the Formless One as "Beloved." The Sikh view is that a separation between male and female denies the wholeness of human nature. Sikh scripture emphasizes instead the significance of being human. In it men and women share human suffering and human hope.

The Guru Granth uses a wide variety of images to show the many ways of con-

necting with the Ultimate One. These images help to make the abstract concept of the Universal Reality concrete and understandable for Sikh believers. For example, the Guru Granth uses images of working people to highlight the dignity of honest labor. The potter with his clay, the blacksmith with his anvil, the woman adorning herself for her loved one, the mother nursing her child, all become metaphors for the relationship of the Universal One to humankind. So too do the animals of the earth, especially those that are domesticated by humans.

The explicit male and female imagery in the Guru Granth does not contradict the formless nature of the Ultimate One. Rather it suggests a vast inclusiveness. The Ultimate Reality is above all and includes all. Whatever human beings can experience in their world is a part of the Ultimate Reality. The varied imagery opens up a range of possibilities for experiencing that Ultimate One.

Sikh women gathering for prayer in a *gurdwara*.

FORM AND FORMLESS

Both physical and metaphysical qualities, form and formlessness, coexist in the Sikh conception of the Ultimate. Guru Arjan says, "Formless and Form It is both, enchanting me so!—"According to Sikh belief the Unknowable is not completely unknown. Bits of It may be gleaned, or gathered, from the varied physical forms of the world. Through various hints human mind and spirit can be launched on a voyage of discovery toward It. Guru Nanak tries to describe the One: "You have a thousand eyes but without eyes you are; you have a thousand forms but without form you are;

Sikhs offering water to members of the community as they enter and leave a prayer room at the Harimandir, the Golden Temple in Amritsar. Service to others, *seva,* is one of the principles of the Sikh religion.

you have a thousand feet, but without feet you are . . ." Human language is not adequate to describe this unique One. In awe the guru exclaims, "I am thoroughly enchanted!"

WITHIN AND ABOVE ALL

In Sikh thought the Ultimate Reality is transcendent, above all else. The cosmos depends on the all-knowing and all-seeing Being for its creation and preservation; but at the same time the Reality is present within all of its creation and is part of the fiber of all being. This suggests to some scholars of religion that the Sikh understanding of the Reality is pantheistic, the God in everything. This view however veers away from the sense of wonder that is at the heart of the Sikh experience of the Ultimate Reality.

At the core of Guru Nanak's awe-inspired message is the understanding that all visible forms are a part of the Formless. Western thinkers like the Greek philosopher Plato have tended to separate ideas and pure forms from the particular examples. In this view only the universal idea of "rose" is real. Particular roses—those that can be seen, smelled, and touched—are changeable and temporary and therefore unreal. The Sikh perspective is to see the particular in the universal and the universal in the particular. Form is formless and vice versa. The Ultimate is within everything and above everything at the same time. For Sikhs the understanding of the Ultimate Reality is a dynamic process. They see a constant, fluid connection between the things of the world and the Ultimate. Because the Ultimate is within everything the world is a joyous place, full of possibility and hope.

A LIGHT IN ALL THE WORLD

The Ultimate Reality presents a paradox, or seeming contradiction: The One is infinite, endless; yet it exists within a finite cosmos, a universe with definite limits. Many verses in the Guru Granth signify the presence of the Ultimate Reality within the world and within all beings:

There is a light in all and the light is That One.

In nature It is seen, in nature heard,
    in nature lies the essence of joy
    and peace
Earth, skies and nether regions
comprise nature
The whole creation is an embodiment
of It.

You are the Primal Being, you are the
Infinite Creator
None can comprehend your limits!
Within each and every being you are,
constantly pervading all.

CHAPTER 5

SIKH ETHICS

Sikh ethics, or code of behavior, can be summed up in Guru Nanak's words: "Truth is higher than all, but higher still is true living." The Mul Mantra named the Infinite One as Truth. Nanak viewed Truth as the highest Reality. Yet his words suggest that it is not enough to know the truth. One must live it as well.

Sikhism regards human life as very precious. All forms of life are worthy of respect, but Sikhs feel that humans are especially favored because they can approach the Divine One. All humans come from the One so all have within them a spark of the Divine. The goal of the Sikh moral code is to help people experience that divine spark within themselves.

THE PROBLEM OF *HAUMAI*

If everyone has a spark of divine Truth within, what keeps people from experiencing it fully? According to Sikhism the root cause of human suffering is *haumai*. *Haumai* literally means "I-myself" and it refers to egotism. Pride, arrogance, and a constant focus on "I" and "me" and "mine" separate the individual from others and from the Universal One. In the Jap, the first hymn Guru

Sikh children in an English *gurdwara* help to serve the *langar* following a wedding celebration. The *langar* is a communal meal cooked by members of the Sikh community which is shared amongst all people present in the *gurdwara*.

Nanak composed, he compares *haumai* to a wall that separates a person from the Universal Reality. An egotistical person's life is marked by competition, malice, ill will toward others, and a craving for power. Blinded by self the person lives for himself or herself alone. Sikhs have a word to describe such a person: *man mukh,* which means "turned toward oneself." In contrast *gur mukh,* "turned toward the guru," describes someone in harmony with the Divine Word.

A person who is full of *haumai* never experiences the joy of the divine spark within. *Haumai* is a chain holding humans in the cycle of death and life.

OVERCOMING *HAUMAI*

How may someone overcome *haumai?* As Sikhs see it external actions like pilgrimages, fasts, and other practices of self-denial are useless. The walls of ego can be broken down, however, by following a simple formula from Guru Nanak's Jap: *sunia, mania man kita bhau*—"hearing, having faith, being full of love."

HEARING THE DIVINE WORD

Sunia literally means "hearing." In the Jap it means listening to the Divine Word. It is the first step on a journey toward unity with the Ultimate Reality.

According to Nanak, through listening come knowledge and wisdom and through listening all suffering and distress lose their power. The sound of the Divine Name, Truth, leads the listener to the ultimate goal: immortality and freedom from the grip of death. The refrain in the Jap repeats that those who hear the Name remain in constant bliss.

Nanak explains that human words are not adequate to explain the Ultimate Reality. However words provide hints of Truth. They are the means of naming, praising, knowing, singing, and discussing the One. People communicate through words and the Ultimate Reality speaks through the words of people. "As the One utters, that is how the words are arranged," the guru says. Hearing the Divine Word is the first step toward living truly.

HAVING FAITH

Mania means "having faith." It is the second step on the spiritual journey. Nanak himself says that this step is hard to define. It is emotional, not intellectual, truth. Faith cannot be discussed or analyzed. However Nanak describes the state of faith as the pathway to freedom, open to everyone. By believing in the Divine Word Sikhs understand that they not only free themselves from the cycle of birth and death, they also help to free other members of the community, their family and friends, who are linked together by the grace of the Ultimate One.

LOVE—THE HIGHEST FORM OF ACTION

Man kita bhau means "to be full of love." This third step goes well beyond hearing the Divine Name and having faith. Love frees those who love from all limitations and barriers. It dissolves the individual ego and opens people to experiencing the other.

A residential community for Sikhs with disabilities built by a Sikh charitable foundation to serve the community's health and education needs. Sikh ethics are ways of expressing love for the Ultimate One. The institutions of *langar, seva, sangat,* and the Khalsa provide an outlet for this love. Acts of love toward all fellow beings show love for the One. Since all are equally children of the One they are treated like kinfolk. The response of love is vital to Sikh philosophy and ethics alike.

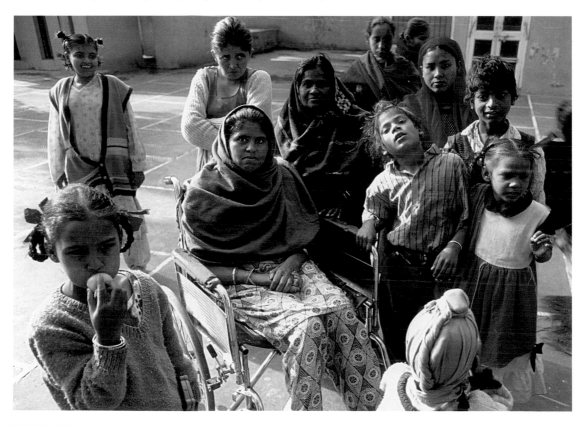

Nanak suggests that love is the highest form of action:

"Those who hear, appropriate and nurture love in their hearts,

They cleanse themselves by bathing at the sacred fount which is within."
— in the Guru Granth

Love purifies the soul. It is essential in Sikh ethics. The Guru Granth applauds love as the supreme virtue:

"They who worship the One with adoring love and thirst for Its True Love,

They who beseechingly cry out—discover peace, for in their heart lies love."

The 10th guru, Gobind Singh, wrote of love as the pathway to the Infinite One. It is a central theme in his composition *Bacitar Natak.* "Only they who love find the Ultimate Reality," he wrote. For the Sikh gurus love is the only path to true liberation: "They who have love within their hearts alone are emancipated"—in Punjabi, *jisu antari priti lagai so mukta.*

POPULAR MORALITY

At the everyday level Sikh morality is best summed up in this maxim: *kirat karni, vand chhakna, te nam japna:* "to labor for one's keep, to share with others, and to practice the repetition of the Divine Name."

KIRAT KARNI

In Punjabi *kirat* means "the labor of one's hands." It is manual work—upright work in pursuit of one's living and is one of the basics of Sikh ethics. The term underscores the dignity of all labor. Sikhs understand it to mean that not to work if one is able is an offense to the faith. Honest work and its satisfactions create a positive attitude toward life. Sikhs reject withdrawal from society. Home and family are the rule.

VAND CHHAKNA

Vand chhakna is the sharing of money and goods before using them oneself. The phrase comes from *vand,* "distribution" or "sharing," and *chhakna,* "to eat." It is based on mutual respect and sharing among equals, not on charity. Just as members of a family share their earnings and goods with one another for the good of the whole, so Sikhs try to act in the larger family of the community for its well-being. This principle of sharing is basic to the institutions of *sangat* and *langar,* which have been primary factors in shaping Sikh conduct.

NAM JAPNA

Nam japna is to remember the Divine Name. *Nam* literally means "name" and *japna,* to "repeat" or "meditate on." Constantly to repeat the name of the One is a great virtue in the Sikh religion. A line in the Guru Granth says *nam* is more important spiritually than other traditionally religious actions: "Superior to all acts of piety, charity, and austerity, is *nam.*" *Nam* does not take the place of other acts but it is the source from which all ethical action comes. According to Guru Amar Das, "Chastity, truth, continence, all are contained in *nam;* without contemplation on *nam,* one does not become pure." Sikhs remind themselves of *nam* throughout the day by repeating the Guru Mantra, *Wahe Guru,* which means "Wonderful Guru" or "God is great."

THE PATH TO ULTIMATE REALITY

In the final lines of the Jap Guru Nanak presents five stages by which human beings can ascend toward the Ultimate Reality. They are a path leading to higher and higher levels of experience. They are the realms, or regions, of duty, knowledge, art, grace, and truth and can be described as follows:

DHARAM KHAND

The first stage is *dharam khand,* the realm of duty. This is the earthly life. It is made up of nights and seasons and dates and days, of time and space. The world contains uncounted varieties of life. "Within this infinite matrix are myriads of species, infinite are their names and forms," says Nanak. Through the Ultimate Reality all are interconnected, and people should live harmoniously with them. Being on earth offers people the opportunity to live ethically and with purpose. Earthly existence is not to be scorned but to be lived fully and intensely. Sikhs believe that actions are important, for whatever someone does has an effect.

GYAN KHAND

The second stage is *gyan khand,* the realm of knowledge. Here the individual becomes aware of the vastness of creation: millions of inhabited planets like Earth, countless mountains, countless moons, suns, and constellations. When someone realizes how limitless creation is he or she also realizes how small human beings are. Knowledge of creation brings with it an awe of the creator. Humility replaces ego. Knowledge destroys limitations and prejudices and creates an all-accepting and all-welcoming attitude.

SARAM KHAND

The third stage, *saram khand*, is the realm of art. Art sharpens and refines human sensibility. In this realm people develop an appreciation of beauty. It is an important stage in the spiritual journey. In Nanak's words, "One who can appreciate fragrance will alone know the flower." Unless they can feel the power of beauty people cannot know the Ultimate Reality, which is there to see, hear, taste, touch, and smell in this world. Sikhs do not distinguish among physical, mental, and spiritual senses. A person has all of these. As Nanak says, "Here are sharpened consciousness, wisdom, mind, and discrimination." The cultivation of the appreciation of beauty opens the way to the next stage of spiritual development.

A Sikh family enjoying a visit to the Taj Mahal in Agra, India. The men in the group are wearing turbans to cover their uncut hair, one of the symbols of membership of the Khalsa.

KARAM KHAND

The fourth stage, *karam khand,* is the realm of grace. Nanak describes it as the home of those who love the One. "Here live warriors and heroes of mighty power," he says. Who are these warriors and heroes? "The true hero," says Nanak, "is one who kills the evil of egotism within." Physical strength and power are not the ideal. Sikhs say, "By conquering oneself, one conquers the world." Indeed they see outer conquests as being much easier than internal ones. Heroines and heroes in this realm of

grace are those who are in control of themselves. They are exempt from the cycle of
birth and death. "They are rejoicing, for
that True One is close to their hearts," says
the guru. Firm in their conviction and full
of joy they ascend to the final stage in their
quest for the Ultimate Reality.

SACH KHAND

The realm of truth, *sach khand,* is the fifth
and highest stage. The opening of the
Guru Granth names the One, *Ikk Oan Kar,*
as "Truth." The realm of truth is the sphere of the One, the home
of the Ultimate Reality. In the home of the Ultimate Reality the
individual and the Divine One merge. The benevolent glance of
the One and the joyful vision of those who seek it come together.
Nanak describes this stage as "hard as iron." It cannot be expressed
in human terms, except as union with infinity. "Here are conti-
nents, constellations, and universes, their counting never ending, never . . ." For the individual there will be no more rebirths
into the world, and no more lives, and no more deaths. The self
is freed from all limitations of space, time, gender, and earthly
considerations. They are replaced by absolute joy.

The Sikh spiritual journey is one of love for fellow beings, the
experience of life in the world, and an insight into beauty. It is not
a journey away from the world. Rather it is grounded in life on
earth. It is on earth that Sikhs work to develop their moral, intellectual, artistic, and spiritual capacities and to catch a glimpse
of the Ultimate Reality. The higher they ascend, the more deeply
they feel that they experience life here and now.

The Realm of Truth

"Truth is higher than all, but higher
still is true living," says Guru Nanak.
Sach khand, the realm of truth, is
the fifth and highest stage by which
human beings can ascend toward
the Ultimate Reality. In this realm
the individual finally reaches true
living. It is the purpose of all human
existence.

CHAPTER 6

RELIGIOUS LIFE AND RITES OF PASSAGE

Whether they live in a traditional community in a Punjabi village or in an ultramodern suburb of Los Angeles or Chicago, Sikhs attempt to connect their every daily activity to their religion.

RELIGIOUS LIFE

A Sikh's first words of greeting reveal the deeply religious dimension of his or her life. When one Sikh meets another each greets the other by placing his or her two hands together, gently bowing, and saying *"Sat Sri Akal,"* which means "Truth is the Timeless One." Their greeting is quite different from the usual Western greeting of shaking hands and calling each other by name. The Sikh greeting combines the second line of the Mul Mantra, "Truth is the Name," and the ideal of Sikh ethics, the last stage of spiritual ascension, unity with the formless One. Instead of speaking their

In a *gurdwara* in Manchester, England, a family gathers for a naming ceremony before the Guru Granth Sahib, the Sikh holy scriptures. The *granthi*, standing in front of the family, recites prayers before the family sit down for the naming ritual.

own names as they greet one another, Sikhs humbly acknowledge the One as their True Reality.

The Sikhs' appearance is noticeably different. Men and teenage boys do not shave their beards or cut their hair. Men and older boys wear the turban, which is made from almost five yards of cloth and comes in many colors. Little boys wear their hair coiled in a topknot with a kerchief tied around it. Male athletes also wear the topknot, since sprinting or other such activities would be difficult to do while wearing a turban.

Uncut hair is one of the five Ks, symbols of the Khalsa, established by Guru Gobind Singh toward the end of the 17th century. Women and girls refrain from cutting their hair as well. Young girls wear long braids and women tie up their hair in a variety of styles. Sikh women dress in a particular style and they can be identified by their clothing—loose trousers called *salvors,* a shirt that reaches to the knees, and a long, sheer scarf wound around the neck or over the head.

On festive occasions the colors of the Sikhs' turbans and scarves are usually quite brilliant. On serious occasions the headgear is usually more somber. Both men and women wear a steel bracelet, *kara,* around the right wrist. The steel of the bracelet symbolizes spiritual courage and strength, and the circle is a reminder of the unity of the Ultimate One, which has no beginning and no end.

Finally, the Sikh second names, Singh for men and Kaur for women, reflect their religion, proclaiming membership in a society of equals and marking them as Sikhs. Sikhs consider all members of the Sikh community to be part of their extended family. Sikhs refer to friends and even distant associates as family members. Parents' friends and associates are referred to as "uncles" and "aunts." Children accept the friends of their brothers and sisters as their own brothers and sisters and the friends of their parents and grandparents as their own parents and grandparents. Until recent times a Punjabi village was regarded as a family unit, and people from the same village were not permitted to marry because the relationship was too close. Throughout their lives Sikhs try to bring others into their own family, breaking down the barriers of caste, race, and religion.

WEAVING RELIGION INTO LIFE

Sikhs weave their religion into their lives. They try to incorporate the spirit of *seva* and *langar* into all their relationships. Sikhs enthusiastically give time and energy to family members, relatives, and friends. Complete strangers who identify themselves as coming from the same village or as having attended the same school or college, or even as being acquainted with a relative's friend, will automatically be showered with hospitality.

In small areas of northern India hotels and inns are practically unknown. Sikh guests, whether invited or not, receive a warm welcome from their host families and are given bedding and food. *Seva,* serving others with a cheerful attitude, is thus a part of everyday life. Sikhs seek jobs for, provide financial assistance to, and extend domestic comfort to fellow Sikhs.

Sikhs who have migrated continue to share their earnings with relatives and friends and their community, though they may be thousands of miles away. They send money home to India for aged parents, for weddings of siblings, for schools and hospitals; in their new home they give to charity and share their Thanksgiving meal with the homeless.

INTEGRATING THE SACRED AND THE SECULAR

Sikhs attempt at all times to integrate the sacred with the secular. They may say their prayers alone, with their families, or with the *sangat,* or congregation, in the *gurdwara.* Morning prayers reverberate through a Sikh home as family members go about their activities. Mothers recite stanzas from the Jap as they prepare breakfast or comb their children's hair. Fathers pray while picking up bedding, cleaning, or gardening. If their home is large

Child Care

In India babysitting is unknown among the Sikhs. Grandparents, aunts, and uncles—whether related by blood or by faith— care for children. Even in such American cities as Los Angeles or Washington, D.C., working parents call on relatives and grandparents originally from the Punjab to help care for children.

enough for a separate worship room a family may gather there in the morning to recite their prayers. Some Sikhs might visit a neighborhood *gurdwara,* thus combining devotions with a morning walk. Others might pray as they drive to work, listen to tapes of scriptural readings, or tune their radios to a Sikh station.

Similarly Sikhs might recite their evening prayers as they tend to various chores or relax on a bicycle ride or a walk. Others might pray in a quiet spot at home or go to the *gurdwara.* Some Sikhs might choose to read the Guru Granth. During certain hours of the day Sikhs who live near a *gurdwara* can hear the prayers and participate from their own lawns or verandas. In the Punjab *kirtan,* or sacred music, is broadcast by radio and television from the Golden Temple in Amritsar, and neighbors often gather to listen to the hymns.

DIVINE PRESENCE IN ALL THINGS

True living for Sikhs involves remembering the One Reality as often and as intimately as possible. The Ultimate Reality is part of time and space. Why should that One not be remembered everywhere and at every moment? From the Sikh perspective daily routine is filled with the Divine Presence. Throughout the course of their daily schedules Sikhs never stop expressing their love for the Divine. *"Wahe Guru"*—"Wonderful Guru"—the Sikhs exclaim, before and after meals, before and after anything they undertake.

Sikhs regularly recite morning prayers called Bani. These "five verses" are Jap, Jaap, Swayyai, Benati Chaupai, and Anand, and they lead the worshipper through the five *khands,* the stages of spiritual development from earthly duty to heavenly bliss. With the meditation on the name of the Ultimate, the five verses form the Nit Nem, "the everyday routine'

Every morning as they prepare for work and school, Sikh family members ask one another, "Have you done your Nit Nem?" In addition Sikhs recite two evening prayers, Rahiras and Kirtan Sohila. Before they begin their prayers Sikhs quiet their minds by repeating the Mul Mantra five times and the Guru Mantra, *Wahe*

Guru, over and over as they meditate on the Ultimate. They also repeat the Guru Mantra many times throughout the day, fulfilling the commandment given to Nanak at the River Bein: "Rejoice in My Name."

THE DAILY PRAYERS

Jap (pronounced JUP) is Guru Nanak's composition. It is the first prayer in the Guru Granth and it expresses the basic philosophy of the Sikhs. Sikhs recite it at dawn, when their minds are fresh and the atmosphere is serene. The Jap describes dawn as the "ambrosial hour," or the "hour of heavenly nectar," and Sikhs feel that it is the best time for hearing the Divine Word.

Jaap (pronounced JAP) and Swayyai are compositions of the 10th guru, Gobind Singh. They appear in his book of poetic com-

Young members of a Sikh family gathered for their morning prayers. The five verses that are said are called Nit Nem—"everyday routine." Even though the young brothers have not yet undergone initiation into the Khalsa, their hair is tied in a cloth knotted at the top.

positions called the Dasam Granth. The Dasam Granth is different from the Guru Granth but Sikhs esteem it highly as the work of Gobind Singh. The Jaap and the Swayyai form an important part of their daily prayers. The Jaap has an energetic sound and rapid rhythm. Repeating it helps Sikhs to focus on the Ultimate Reality described in Nanak's Jap, and sets the tone for the day.

Swayyai are quatrains, or four-line rhymes. The 10 Swayyai that Sikhs include in their daily prayers also come from the Dasam Granth. These rhymes stress devotion as the essence of religion. They reject all forms of external worship and express Nanak's message of love. Sikhs also recite the Swayyai during the *amrita* ceremony, or initiation into the Khalsa and the fellowship of the Sikhs.

Benati Chaupai, or "supplication in quatrains" by Gobind Singh begs the help and protection of the Universal One. With the words "I beg that I keep remembering you" Sikhs ask never to be allowed to forget the name of the Ultimate. They also ask that they be saved from evil and that their people be happy and free.

Anand, or "bliss," by Guru Amar Das, represents the end of the spiritual journey. It expresses the hope for union with the One and for the joy of being forever in the realm of truth. Before they begin their prayers Sikhs quiet their minds by repeating the Mul Mantra five times and the Guru Mantra, *Wahe Guru,* over and over as they meditate on the Ultimate. They also repeat the Guru Mantra many times throughout the day, fulfilling the commandment received by Guru Nanak: "Rejoice in My Name."

Rahiras is part of the evening service. It consists of hymns from Guru Nanak, Guru Ram Das, and Guru Arjan. The Benati Chaupai is also a part of this evening prayer. The Rahiras ends with stanzas from the Anand. Summer and winter Sikhs recite Rahiras at dusk, just as the day and the night come together. Through the Rahiras Sikhs show their respect for the transcendent Reality. They sing the praises of the Divine, seek the protection of the all-powerful One, and express their joy at hearing the Word within themselves.

THE *BHOG* CEREMONY

The word *bhog* literally means "pleasure." It is similar to the Greek word *eucharist*, which means "thanksgiving" and, in the spiritual sense, refers to the Christian sacrament of Holy Communion. *Bhog* involves reading the concluding pages of the Guru Granth and sharing the Sikh sacrament of *karahprasad*, which concludes every religious ceremony.

Bhog can take place anywhere—in a room in someone's home, in a public hall, or in a *gurdwara*. Its leaders are members of the Sikh congregation and both men and women may lead. People gather around the Guru Granth and usually everyone sits on the floor, facing the holy text.

KARAHPRASAD

Members of the community prepare *karahprasad*, the sweet sacrament, which consists of equal parts of butter, flour, and sugar prepared in a large steel pot over a wood fire or on a coal, electric, or gas burner. During its preparation Sikhs remain in an attitude of reverence, with their heads covered and their feet bare, and they recite hymns from the Guru Granth. When the *karahprasad* is ready it is put in a large, flat dish and covered with a clean cloth. Then one of the leaders respectfully lifts it and carries it on his or her head to the congregation. The steaming *karahprasad*, with its rich aroma, is placed on the right side of the Guru Granth.

KIRTAN SOHILA—THE HYMN OF PRAISE

Kirtan Sohila consists of five hymns and is the ending to evening prayers. Sikhs recite it as the holy book is closed before they go to bed. It is also recited at cremations or funerals. The first three hymns are by Guru Nanak. They are followed by one each from Guru Ram Das and Guru Arjan. The first hymn speaks of the union of the individual self with the Ultimate Reality. The second presents the oneness of the Ultimate, in spite of the great diversity of scriptures, teachers, and philosophies in the world. The third rejects external piety and ritual. It portrays the cosmos worshipping in harmony—the skies, sun, moon, and stars, and all growing things are an offering to the Divine. The fourth hymn, by Ram Das, explains how the sound of the Divine Name eases all suffering and ends the cycle of death and birth. The fifth hymn, by Arjan, celebrates life on earth. It invites people to take the opportunity of life to serve others and win merit. It promises that the person who comes to know the Divine Mystery will enjoy the bliss and freedom of spiritual immortality.

KIRTAN—SACRED HYMNS

During *bhog* a group of musicians usually sings hymns from the Guru Granth. A reader reads the inaugural hymn and then slowly begins to chant the last five pages of the Guru Granth. These pages begin with 57 couplets by the ninth guru, Tegh Bahadur, and are followed by the *mundavani,* the seal of Guru Arjan, which stamps the Guru Granth as a platter holding the three important delicacies of Truth, Contentment, and Contemplation. All who are present are invited to partake of and savor the sacrament.

THE ARDAS

After the reading the entire congregation stands. With hands folded and heads bowed they recite the Ardas, the prayer of supplication. In this prayer Sikhs remember the Ultimate Reality. They recall their first 10 gurus and the embodiment of their spirit in the Guru Granth. They also remember events of Sikh heroism, devotion, and martyrdom. The leading member of the gathering, or any other person who can read the Gurmukhi script of the Guru Granth, begins the Ardas, and the congregation joins in, exclaiming *"Wahe Guru"*—"Wonderful Guru."

Toward the end of the Ardas the leader asks the congregation for a special blessing. Each reading of the Guru Granth is undertaken for a special purpose, and the blessing of the day recalls that purpose. The Ardas ends with the whole congregation praying for the prosperity and happiness of all humanity. While wishing for the good of all, the Sikhs bow in front of their sacred text touching their foreheads to the ground, and then seat themselves on the floor in front of their holy book. Then the reader opens the Guru Granth and reads the hymn at the top of the left-hand page to obtain the *hukm,* or Divine Command, for the day. The congregation then interprets the passage chosen from in the Guru Granth in the context of the special purpose of the day's service.

RITES OF PASSAGE

The Guru Granth is read for all rites of passage, for any family event, or for blessings on a new job or house. The readings differ:

Family members and Sikh musicians playing for the bride and groom after their wedding service and *langar* meal in a *gurdwara*. Sikh marriages mark an important union between two families and celebrations will continue at a family home or in a venue hired for the occasion.

The *bhog* thanksgiving service ends with the distribution of *karahprasad*. Each member of the congregation receives a warm, buttery handful of this Sikh sacrament in his or her outstretched palms. The sacrament is distributed to all, regardless of religious affiliation. Many times *langar*, the community meal, follows the *bhog* ceremony. The members of the congregation stand, bow before the Guru Granth, and walk outside to the lawn or into another room where *langar* is being served. Some seat themselves in long rows on the floor to partake of the meal, while others help with the cooking, serving, and cleaning up.

Members of a congregation receiving *karahprasad,* the Sikh sacrament.

they may be continuous for 48 hours or they may be any slower variation thereof. And all Sikh ceremonies culminate with the *bhog* ceremony. The prescribed forms for Sikh rituals relating to baptism, marriage, and death appear in the *Sikh Rahit Maryada,* or "Book of Ethical Codes."

NAME-GIVING

In Sikhism there are no taboos surrounding childbirth. Guru Nanak and his successors rejected the generally accepted notion in the India of their day that a household was impure, or unclean, for 40 days after the birth of a child. (In traditional India the home in which a girl was born was considered impure longer than the home in which a boy was born.) However the Sikh gurus regarded the birth of any child, boy or girl, as a divine gift.

Parents take their baby for his or her first visit to the *gurdwara* as soon as such a visit is suitable. During their visit the family offers money and silk coverings for the Guru Granth. Sometimes the family requests that the Guru Granth be fully read during the baby's first visit. Devout families often request that the baby be baptized in the *amrita* ceremony, and the person performing the ceremony prepares the *amrita* by mixing sugar with water and reading five stanzas of the Jap. After the concluding prayer a few drops of *amrita* are placed in the child's mouth. The mother drinks the rest of the *amrita.*

Although the birth of a child is a major event, birthday parties in Sikh life are usually quiet family affairs. Families celebrate by reciting *kirtan,* reading from the Guru Granth, and preparing *langar.* Wealthy families, however, may have big gatherings for children, almost like wedding celebrations.

Name-Giving Ceremony

The name-giving ceremony concludes with the following prayer:

I present this child and with Your Grace
I administer the amrita
(nectar of immortality)
May the child grow up to be a true Sikh
Devoting the self to the service of others
and the Motherland.
May the child be inspired with devotion,
May the holy food be acceptable
to the Guru
By the ever-increasing glory of the
Divine Name
May the whole creation be blessed.

(In Sir Jogerndra Singh, *Sikh Ceremonies.*)

CHOOSING A NAME

The timing and organization of the name-giving ceremony depend on the wishes of the parents. They choose a name by consulting the Guru Granth. While the spine of the Guru Granth rests on the cushions, a reader holds the holy book closed with both hands and then gently lets it open at random. The child receives a name beginning with the first letter at the top of the left-hand page of the Guru Granth. Sikhs do not often have different first names for boys and girls. The addition of the name Kaur or Singh indicates the gender of the child. At this time the child also receives his or her first *kara,* or steel bracelet. Musicians then recite hymns of thanksgiving. A popular hymn for name-giving ceremonies contains these words: "May you have the felicitations of your father and mother and may you always remember the name of the Ultimate Provider." After the hymns the Ardas prayer is said and the sacrament of *karah-prasad,* a mixture made of equal amounts of flour, sugar, water, and butter, is distributed to all.

Baby receiving *amrita,* a mixture of sugar and water, during a name-giving ceremony.

AMRITA INITIATION

Amrita initiation is the reenactment of the ceremony that took place when the Khalsa was established by Guru Gobind Singh in 1699. *Amrita* is a Sanskrit word meaning "immortal," and it traditionally describes the nectar of immortality. In Sikhism, however, *amrita* is not some magical potion that leads to immortality. Rather it signifies an inner experience of Ultimate Oneness. For the Sikh initiation ceremony *amrita* is prepared by mixing water and sugar with a double-edged sword while prayers are chanted. *Amrita* combines clarity of mind, represented by water; sweetness of character, represented by sugar; military valor, represented by the sword; and a poetic spirituality, represented by the chanting of the sacred verses. The divine nectar introduces the individual into the Khalsa, the casteless society with its belief in the One Infinite Reality.

The Age of Initiation

Amrita initiation, or baptism, is open to all. "Any man or woman of whatever nationality, race, or social standing who is prepared to accept the rules governing the Sikh community has the right to receive *amrita* initiation," says the *Sikh Rahit Maryada*. No particular age is prescribed for initiation. It may be as soon as a boy or a girl is old enough to be able to read the scripture and comprehend the articles of the Sikh faith. Or it may be later in life—some people even wait until their own children are grown.

CONDUCTING THE *AMRITA* CEREMONY

Amrita initiation can take place at any age. As with all Sikh ceremonies, the *amrita* initiation does not have to take place in the *gurdwara*. It may be conducted virtually anywhere, but it is usually held in a quiet, enclosed room. The Guru Granth and a reader must be present. Any five Sikhs who are already members of the Khalsa can administer the ceremony. The five fill a steel bowl with clean water and sugar, kneel on the right knee as if ready for battle, and recite the Jap, Jaap, Swayyai, Chaupai, and Anand. As they recite these five prayers, the five stir the water and sugar with a small sword. After the prayers, one of the five says the Ardas. Then the *amrita* is served. The five drink the *amrita* from their cupped hands and sprinkle some on their eyes and hair. The initiates receive the holy liquid five times, each time saying *"Wahe guru ji ka khalsa wahe guru ji ki fateh,*" "The Khalsa belongs to the Wonderful Guru and victory belongs to the Wonderful Guru."

LIVING AS KHALSA SIKHS

After the ceremony they all share the ambrosial nectar, all sipping from the same bowl. Then together they recite Guru Nanak's Mul Mantra and the Guru Mantra, *Wahe Guru,* remembering the One Singular Reality. The initiates are told that they are now children of Guru Gobind Singh and his wife Mata Sahib Kaur. Their historical and spiritual parentage makes them all brothers and sisters, and they are to live as Khalsa Sikhs. Thus they are to maintain the principles of the Guru Granth and their physical identity through the five Ks. They are not to eat the meat of an animal killed by ritual slaughter. The distinctive Sikh rite of *amrita* initiation concludes with *karahprasad.*

MARRIAGE

Marriage is regarded as an important rite of passage in every society, but for the Sikhs it is a means of serving the Divine Reality and fellow humanity. Sikhs feel that people best fulfill their individual potential within marriage. All Sikh gurus—with the exception of Guru Har Krishan, who had a short life—were married. Marriage between children, once a common practice in India, is forbidden. Divorce is legal and both men and women can remarry. Remarriage of widows is an accepted practice as well.

Like those of most Indian couples Sikh marriages, both in India and in Western countries, are arranged, usually by the couple's parents. Great care is taken in choosing partners, and no person is made to marry against his or her will. Marriage arrangements may be made anytime after a young person turns 18; often families wait until a prospective bride or groom has finished college or become established in a career. If the couple are from the same locality they may know each other, but this is often not the case. Sikhs see marriage not only as the uniting of two people but also as the uniting of two families, and the marriage takes place with the advice and assistance of the extended family on both sides.

ENGAGEMENT

Many Sikhs weave customs into their wedding celebrations that are not specifically part of the Sikh religion but rather are a part of Punjabi culture.

A formal engagement is not necessary in Sikh life, but if the two parties wish it the engagement takes place before the Guru Granth in the future groom's house. The ceremony is thus different from a simple exchange of rings between the couple. In a Sikh engagement the prospective groom and bride do not meet; the bride's relatives and friends take gifts of sweet foods, dried fruits, money, a bracelet *(kara)*, and sometimes a ring to the home of the groom. When the bride's group arrives the groom's family takes them to the Guru Granth, and they place their gifts in front of the book. The two families sing scriptural hymns together and the bride's father then presents their gifts to the prospective groom, who takes a bit of the dried fruit *(chhuhara,* or date), signifying acceptance of the match and the gifts. The families then wave money around the groom's head to symbolize a prosperous life. Later the money is given to charity. The ceremony ends with the recitation of the Ardas and the taking of *hukm.*

This ceremony is often followed by one in the bride's home, in which the groom's family offers a *chunni charauna,* or red head scarf, to the bride-to-be, accompanied by jewelry, clothes, sweet foods, and other gifts, including a red thread to be braided into the bride's hair. The red head scarf is to be worn by the bride at the engagement ceremony. To people in the East, red is the color of good fortune. The sign of blood and life, red is also the color of the Sikh bridal outfit. During the engagement the bride, with her female relatives, has her own celebration with her female relatives, who paint her hands with henna, a reddish-brown dye obtained from the leaves of a henna plant, and sing songs and dance together.

BEFORE THE WEDDING

One to three days prior to the wedding the prospective bride and the groom observe separate periods of seclusion. Both avoid dressing up and going out but their homes resound with joy and music. In the evenings female friends and relatives on both sides gather and sing songs to the accompaniment of a drum. While the lead singer plays the drum placed beneath her knee, her companion beats on the wooden center with a spoon and the others sing Punjabi folk songs. The songs on the groom's side are called *ghorian,* and those on the bride's side are called *suhag.* The singers may make up songs on the spot. Often a team of young girls competes against a team of older women, and the competition is vigorous.

On the eve of the wedding both bride and groom take ritual baths in their respective homes. Each is given a massage with a mixture of flour, turmeric, and milk. A traditional version of a modern bath scrub, the mixture leaves the skin light and clean. This rite of purification is accompanied by song, music, and clapping. After the bath each puts on new clothes. From her maternal relatives the bride receives a headband, a nose ring, ivory bracelets, clothes, and utensils. The bride's family also provides new outfits for the groom and his family.

THE DAY OF THE WEDDING

Before the groom and his party leave for the marriage ceremony at the bride's home they observe several rituals. First they recite the Ardas. Then comes *sihra bandhi,* a ceremony in which the eldest sister ties a *sihra,* a shining veil made of gilded strings with a plume on top, around the groom's forehead. In return for this tying, or *bandhi,* the sister receives money from the groom. Then the groom's eldest sister-in-law (his brother's wife) puts kohl—a dark cosmetic-like eye shadow—around the groom's eyes.

In the meantime the mare on which the groom will travel to the bride's home is fed with barley and *gram,* a flour mixture. The sister decorates the mare and braids her reins with red thread. Just as everything is complete and the groom is ready to proceed, the groom's sister takes the reins of the horse and jokingly demands gifts from her brother, and the groom gives money to his sisters and cousins. A younger brother or a nephew or cousin

CIRCLING THE GURU GRANTH

The Sikh marriage ceremony is known as *anand karag*, which literally means "blissful occasion," and in which the groom and bride circle the Guru Granth four times as the wedding hymns are chanted. This is a legal ceremony as well as a religious one. It was officially recognized as such by the Sikh Marriage Act of 1909. *Anand karag* can be traced back to the time of the third guru,

Amar Das (1552–74), who is the author of the 40-stanza hymn called Anand. Six stanzas from this hymn form a part of the Sikhs' daily prayers, and the complete Anand is recited on all important occasions. The Lavan, meaning "circling," a hymn in four stanzas, was composed by the fourth guru. Ram Das (1574–81), and is also an important part of the Sikh wedding ceremony.

The bride and groom approaching the Guru Granth, which they will walk around four times during the marriage ceremony.

of the groom acts as the best man, and as the procession begins he sits behind the groom on the horse.

When they reach the bride's home a formal meeting of the two families takes place. This meeting is called *milni*. The bride's party receives the groom's party by chanting hymns of welcome.

Ardas is said. Introductions follow. The father of the groom is introduced to the father of the bride, the mother to the mother, brother to brother, uncle to uncle, and friend to friend. Each family member meets the other with a welcoming embrace. Often members of the bride's family give gifts such as blankets and jewelry to the family of the groom. Once again the members of the wedding party wave money around one another's heads. Then the wedding group makes its way toward the Guru Granth.

ANAND KARAJ

The *anand karaj,* or marriage ceremony, can take place in a *gurdwara* or at home on a terrace, in a courtyard, in a drawing room—anywhere, so long as the Guru Granth is present. The ceremony begins with the singing of scriptural hymns. While *kirtan,* the musical recitations, are going on the guests and hosts assemble. After bowing, the groom sits down before the holy book. The bride, accompanied by her friends and relatives, joins him and sits on his left. The opening Ardas is said. This time, with the exception of the couple and their respective parents or guardians, the entire congregation is seated. Blessings are sought for the couple. Musicians sing a passage from the Guru Granth recounting how one rejoices and tastes nectar in the company of saints.

A scholar or a politician next makes a formal speech, addressing the couple and explaining the significance of Sikh marriage. The speaker reminds the couple of their obligations, not only toward each other but also toward their families, their community, and society at large. Usually the speaker reiterates Guru Amar Das's emphasis on marriage as a "union of the divine spark" rather than as a civil or social contract. In the Guru Granth the fourth guru says, "They are not husband and wife who sit side by side next to each other; only they are truly wedded who personify one single spirit in two bodies."

LINKING THE COUPLE

After the speech the bride's father unites the bride and groom with a saffron-colored scarf. He places one end of the scarf in the groom's hands, passes it over the groom's shoulder, and places the other end in the bride's hand. The musicians recite a scriptural verse that urges the bride to ignore all empty praise and slander and be totally attached to the bond symbolized by the scarf. This rite of linking the couple together is a physical representation of the spiritual union mentioned in the Guru Granth. Tied with the scarf, husband and wife together are to renounce all evil and devote themselves fully to the Ultimate Reality. However, many Sikhs take this rite to mean that the daughter is no longer a part of her parents' family and henceforth belongs entirely to her husband and her husband's family. It is a poignant, moving, and solemn moment.

READING THE LAVAN

The actual marriage ceremony begins with the opening of the Guru Granth and the reading of the Lavan, which describes marriage as a rite of passage into higher and higher circles of existence. As each verse is recited and sung the couple reverentially circle the Guru Granth in a clockwise direction. To show their support relatives help the couple as they circuit the holy book. During the fourth stanza the entire congregation showers the bride and groom with flower petals as a sign of rejoicing. The ceremony concludes with the customary singing of passages from Anand and the recitation of Ardas, this time with the entire congregation standing. Finally *hukm,* the divine command, is received from the Guru Granth, and *karahprasad,* the sweet sacrament, is served to the entire congregation.

In different parts of the world Sikhs have adopted a variety of ceremonies. However essentially the religious ceremony is simple, consisting of circling the Guru Granth four times. Before and after each circuit the couple bows before the Guru Granth. This gesture is symbolic of their marriage consent and their commitment to each other. No vows are exchanged, no kisses are given, no legal materials are signed or witnessed. The four circlings and the recitations of the Lavan constitute the Sikh marriage, a marriage that is both religious and legal.

DOLI

The marriage ceremony is followed by a festive lunch. Yet the joyous mood soon changes to one of sadness: the bride must leave her parents' home. Amid farewell songs and tears the bride departs with the groom's party to his home. Her departure is called *doli*, which refers to the traditional Indian marriage procession in which the bride was carried on a palanquin, a covered seat atop two poles. Today the means of transportation varies from horse carts to decorated limousines. Relatives and friends greet the bride at the other end, and then many other rites are performed, such as pouring oil on the threshold, circulating a bowl of water around the couple's heads, and eating rice and grains.

DEATH

In Sikhism life and death are regarded as natural processes. According to the Guru Granth just as each day that dawns must reach its end, so must all people depart. For Sikhs death does not

Sikh men and boys dancing at a celebration following a wedding ceremony. The groom is in the center of the group with golden decorations around his turban and neck to which gifts of money have been attached. In modern Sikh families the groom's family gives a wedding reception and the couple cuts the wedding cake.

mean an absolute end. The Sikh gurus and their scripture stress the moral, intellectual, and spiritual refinement of the individual; their concern is with development here and now. The Sikh ideal is to attain infinity and immortality; the objective is to become part of the Ultimate Reality. As a result, when the physical, finite existence ends it is not viewed as a final terminating point.

A PEACEFUL DEPARTURE

Sikhs believe that when a person is about to die his or her attention is drawn toward the Ultimate. No worldly sorrows or grief should intrude on the peaceful departure. External signs of grief such as weeping, wailing, or beating one's breasts and thighs, which are quite common in northern India, are forbidden in Sikh life. Sikh life is intergenerational, with young couples, their children, parents, and grandparents often living under one roof. The elderly are not consigned to homes for the aged; they grow old and die at home. Thus even the youngest Sikh children become

RETURNING TO THE FOUR ELEMENTS

Sikhs cremate their dead. Guru Nanak himself was not concerned with whether his body would be cremated or buried or floated down the river, so his followers adopted cremation for practical reasons. Since Sikhs believe that the body is made up of four elements and that during cremation it returns to the four elements, cremation also seems to be more natural. Fire merges with the fire that is lighted, the earth goes to the earth, the air to the air, and the ashes and the bones (called *phul,* literally, "flowers") are immersed in running water, signifying the return of the fourth element to water itself.

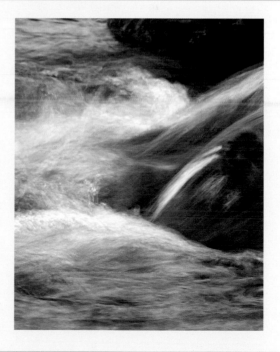

Cremated ashes and bones are immersed in running water to symbolize a return to the elements.

familiar with death, and as adults they accept death more matter-of-factly than do many people in the West, where death occurs mostly in hospitals and nursing homes.

When someone dies early in life or from some unnatural cause, people demonstrate their grief. However when the elderly die—especially those who have lived a long and happy life, witnessing the birth of children and grandchildren—grief is muted. Death is presumed to be a stage that completes the liberation of the soul, and Sikhs sing praises to the Ultimate. The body is carried in a procession with musicians playing and singing, a ritual that is reminiscent of the bridegroom going to wed his bride.

FUNERAL RITUALS AND BLESSINGS

When a person dies the body is bathed and dressed in clean clothes. A young woman is often dressed in her bridal clothes, another connection between death and marriage. The body is covered with white sheets, placed on a bier, or platform, and carried to the cremation ground on the shoulders of four people closest to the deceased. As the funeral procession moves mourners recite passages from the Guru Granth. When the mourners reach the cremation ground, they place the body on a platform of firewood.

A close relative lights the funeral pyre, or fire, and then those present recite the evening hymn, Kirtan Sohila.

A funeral is a rite of passage just as a marriage ceremony is. The oil of blessing is poured out in both rituals. This scriptural verse attempts to overcome the fear of death. It presents death as something all share and as a passage that opens people into a union with the Transcendent Reality. Following the Kirtan Sohila Ardas is offered, seeking blessing for the departed soul. When the party returns from the cremation ground all wash themselves, and *karahprasad* is distributed. Taking *karah-*

Praising the Eternal Reality

Even during one's last journey on earth, the Sikh is called on to recognize and praise the Eternal Reality by singing the following hymn found in the Guru Granth:

Wake up my mind, wake up from the oblivion of sleep
The body that came with you will soon bid you goodbye . . .
Says Nanak, sing the praise of the Ultimate One
For all else is an ephemeral dream . . .

prasad, which is normally a very joyous event, serves to declare that grief must end and normal life must return once more

As soon as it can be conveniently arranged, the reading of the Guru Granth is begun by the family members. The *bhog* ceremony takes place on the 10th day with the *antam* Ardas (the final Ardas) recited on behalf of the deceased. Visitors wear white, black, and earth colors, more brilliant colors being reserved for weddings and other festive occasions. Thereafter people continue to visit the family members of the dead person. They do not necessarily exchange words, but they sit in silence to share their grief and to commemorate their loss.

Sikhs generally do not pay much attention to birthdays or wedding anniversaries, but death anniversaries of their loved ones are important. They continue to commemorate these occasions annually through *bhog* ceremonies. They keep the memory of the deceased alive by making gifts to the needy, to schools, libraries, and hospitals, and to the *gurdwara* itself. This final rite of passage is the most significant of them all, for it represents the ultimate stage on the path toward union with the Supreme Being.

The Evening Hymn

The evening hymn that is sung at funerals is also the one sung at the end of the day and uses the symbol of a wedding to recall union with the Ultimate:

The day of my wedding is fixed,
In unison, O friends, pour ritual oil.
Bless me that I unite with my Groom.
From home to home these summons are received daily
Remember the Summoner, O friends, for this day must come to one and all.

—Kirtan Sohila

CHAPTER 7

SACRED SPACE AND ALTERED TIME

According to the Guru Granth, "Paradise is where the Ultimate Reality is praised." For Sikhs, wherever the Guru Granth is, that space is sacred. Whenever the Guru Granth is read, seen, remembered, or recited, that time is sacred. Certain days are more historically significant, however, and certain places have a value that comes from their association with the gurus or from their appeal to the senses.

The *gurdwara*, the Sikh place of worship, is, literally, a "door" (*dwara*) to ultimate enlightenment (*guru*). As much as possible the *gurdwara* is designed to invite worshippers to feel the presence of the Transcendent Reality. It provides large areas of open space so that people do not feel confined, and its outward appearance and size can vary. A *gurdwara* may be a single room in a private home;

Children dressed to celebrate the festival of Baisakhi. It is a day of religious observances but also a day of festivities when crowds gather to watch colorful processions and musical performances. Important academic functions also take place on Baisakhi. New books are released, and scholars receive awards. The Khalsa community initiates new members on this birthday of the Khalsa itself. At *gurdwaras,* a new yellow Sikh flag replaces the old one. Overall Baisakhi is regarded as a good time for all kinds of new beginnings.

a simple, rustic structure in a small village; or a sumptuous, multistoried building, surrounded by a reflecting pool, in a large city. Any available hall or dwelling can be adapted and people often meet in private homes.

One identifying mark of a *gurdwara* is the flag that flies over it. Even from a distance the flag, which is yellow in color, triangular in shape, and emblazoned with the emblem of the Sikh Khalsa, can be easily recognized. The emblem, a double-edged sword surrounded by two semicircular swords, can also be seen on the *gurdwara*'s walls, windows, and doors.

A *gurdwara* has four doors, indicating welcome to people of all castes. Within there is no altar or special holy place. The Guru Granth rests on a platform, the focus of attention. There are no statues or pictures that represent the Ultimate Reality in any form. The congregation can gather inside or outside the *gurdwara*—it does not really matter. There are no chairs or pews; all members sit on large mats spread on the floor. Women and men sit separately by tradition.

In India a *gurdwara* can be easily recognized by its white domes and minarets, or towers, leading the eye toward the sky. A large courtyard within the *gurdwara* contributes to a feeling of openness. Many *gurdwaras* have a reflecting pool and people bathe in its waters, sit near it to pray, or walk around it in contemplation. The *gurdwaras* in Asia are often modeled after the most sacred of all Sikh holy places, Harimandir, the Golden Temple at Amritsar in India, and many are of historical note and are places of pilgrimage.

THE GOLDEN TEMPLE

Harimandir, the Golden Temple, is the central shrine of the Sikhs. Sikh ritual and ceremony took form there. The temple is an example of the fundamental characteristics of Sikh art and architecture.

The Golden Temple rests on a platform in the middle of a sacred reflecting pool. Guru Ram Das originally built the pool in 1577 and named it Amritsar, or "pool of nectar." When Arjan

MARBLE SPLENDOR

A reflecting pool surrounding the Golden Temple lies like a peaceful oasis in the midst of the crowded, narrow streets of the city of Amritsar, which grew up around it. The pool is surrounded on four sides by a wide marble walkway, which in turn is enclosed by a white marble portico, or covered porch, several stories high, with a doorway on each side. The upper half of the building is covered in gold-plated copper sheets, giving the temple its name. At the southern side of the building are steps leading to the pool. Visitors descend the steps to obtain water from the pool. They might drink the water, sprinkle it on themselves, or fill bottles to take home to friends and relatives, especially the sick.

Sikhs walking on the marble walkway surrounding the reflecting pool at the center of which sits the Golden Temple.

succeeded to the guruship he had the temple built in the sacred pool. Guru Arjan wanted this first Sikh shrine to be different from other places of worship. Thus instead of ascending stairs, worshippers descend stairs to the Golden Temple in humility. According to historical accounts a Muslim, Miran Mir, laid the first foundation stone of the Sikh temple, once again reinforcing the Sikh principle that all faiths are different expressions of the One Ultimate Reality.

CONTINUAL READINGS

Both inside and out the temple is covered with beautifully intricate carvings. The temple is never silent; sacred music plays 22 hours out of 24. In the center of the ground floor the Guru Granth rests under a jewel-studded canopy on silk and brocade cloth. From a second-floor balcony *granthis*, or readers, take turns reading from the holy book. Before a reader ends his or her period of reading the replacement reader steps in and the two *granthis* read a few words in unison. In this way recitation of the holy word never stops. In addition readings of the Guru Granth may be taking place on other levels of the temple at the same time.

DECORATION AND LAYOUT

The second story of the Golden Temple forms a sort of balcony with windows on either side. One set of windows looks outward toward the sacred pool and the town, while the other opens to the Guru Granth on the floor below. The ceilings and walls are inlaid with mirrors; every solid surface is decorated with delicate designs. The third floor consists of an open-air walkway. In the center is a small square pavil-

---

A Pool of "Ambrosial Waters"

For Sikhs the Golden Temple represents the highest attainment of beauty and tranquillity. Guru Arjan himself installed the Guru Granth there on August 16, 1604. When the Guru Granth was opened at random on that day it revealed the following commandment:

Beautiful is this spot, beautiful is this pool filled with ambrosial waters;
Nectar flows, the wonderful task has been accomplished,
All desires have been fulfilled.
Joy pervades the world, all suffering has ended.

To Sikhs the scriptural verse appropriately and auspiciously expresses the beauty of this sacred place at Amritsar, the holiest shrine of the Sikhs.

Sikh pilgrims bathing in the sacred pool, a source of physical and spiritual refreshment. The sacred reflecting pool was built by Guru Ram Das in 1577 who gave it the name, Amritsar or "pool of nectar."

ion topped by a golden dome. Visitors often pause to feed the birds that stop to rest there.

In addition to the Golden Temple the five *takhts,* or seats of temporal authority, are of major importance. In those places Sikh leaders traditionally made decisions about the secular, or nonreligious, and religious aspects of Sikhism.

THE AKAL TAKHT

The Akal Takht, or "Throne of the Formless," at Amritsar faces the Golden Temple. Sikhs regard it as the supreme seat of religious and temporal authority. Its foundation was originally laid in 1609 under the direction of Guru Hargobind. By that act the sixth guru took community affairs out of the Golden Temple, reserving the temple for prayer and worship.

Guru Hargobind himself presided over important religious, social, and political gatherings at the Akal Takht. He held a court of justice and many Sikhs went there to have their grievances heard and resolved. Over the centuries additions expanded the Akal Takht into a five-story building with a golden dome and intricate interior decorations. This historic building was severely damaged in June 1984 when the Indian Army fired on Sikhs assembled inside. A significant number of innocent worshippers were killed.

Large numbers of Sikhs still assemble before the Akal Takht. The sound of a kettledrum announces the ceremonial activities that take place there. In the morning and the evening the personal weapons of the Sikh gurus are displayed. The two most prized are the swords of Hargobind and Gobind Singh. Sikh leaders continue to proclaim formal Sikh policy from the halls of the *takht.* A saffron robe of honor conferred at the Akal Takht is a mark of great respect. It is

Five Seats of Authority

The five seats of temporal authority for Sikhs are the Akal Takht, Patna Sahib, Keshgarh Sahib, Hazur Sahib, and Damdama Sahib. Several of these places are associated with Sikh history, especially with the life of the 10th guru, Gobind Singh.

given to those who render extraordinary service to the Sikh community.

PATNA SAHIB

The city of Patna is located 500 miles east of Delhi on the Ganges River. Both Guru Nanak and Siddhartha Gautama, Lord Buddha, the central figure of the Buddhist faith, are said to have visited there. Patna is also the birthplace of Gobind Singh and a shrine there commemorates his birth. The shrine, in one of the old quarters of Patna, was originally the mansion of Salis Rai Johri, a follower of Guru Nanak. To show his devotion to the Sikh faith he converted his home into an inn that was free for travelers and pilgrims. Guru Tegh Bahadur stayed there when he visited Patna. Later a magnificent house was built above the inn. Eventually this building came to be known as the shrine Takht Sri Harmandir Sahib.

Relics of Guru Gobind Singh are preserved in this shrine. His sword, four arrows, and a pair of his sandals are displayed along with some of his writings and those of his father, which are collected into a book.

Queen Mania and the Boy Gobind

Gobind Singh, the son of Guru Tegh Bahadur, spent his early years in Patna and many stories are told of his childhood there. One is about a queen named Mania, who was very sad because she had no children. She saw little Gobind, who was only four years old at the time, and she wished that she had a child of her own. The boy promised that he would be like a son to her. They became friends and Mania gave him grain. Today grain is still served in the *langar* at Patna Sahib in recognition of the friendship between the boy Gobind and Queen Mania.

KESHGARH SAHIB

The town of Anandpur—literally the "town of joy" (*anand*)—is located in the foothills of the Himalayas in the Shivalik valley of northern India. There Takht Keshgarh Sahib is a monument to the founding of the Khalsa by Guru Gobind Singh. The shrine is constructed at the place where the 10th guru administered *amrita*, or Sikh baptism, to his five beloved Sikhs. Each year Sikhs reenact the founding of the Khalsa in Anandpur.

Other historically significant *gurdwaras* are located near Keshgarh Sahib. Gurdwara Guru ka Mahal, for instance, was built by

The Keshgarh Sahib at Anandpur, northern India, marks the place where Guru Gobind Singh founded the Khalsa and is a place of pilgrimage for many Sikhs.

the ninth guru, Tegh Bahadur, as his home. Guru Gobind Singh's two sons, the grandsons of Tegh Bahadur, were born there. Guru Tegh Bahadur was beheaded under the Mughal rule in Delhi in 1675. Soon after, his follower Jaita carried the guru's head to Anandpur, where it was burned to ash, and the Gurdwara Sisganj (*sis* means "head") was built there to commemorate the event. The shrine in Delhi that marks the place of Guru Tegh Bahadur's martyrdom is also known as Gurdwara Sisganj.

SRI HAZUR SAHIB

Takht Sri Hazur Sahib in south central India is the site of the death of the 10th guru, Gobind Singh. It is located in Nanded in the state of Maharashtra. Maharaja Ranjit Singh, a great Sikh king, directed its construction between 1832 and 1837. It is a two-story *gurdwara;* both its architecture and its interior decoration are modeled after the Golden Temple. On the first floor recitations from the Guru Granth take place continually, day and night.

The *gurdwara's* treasury contains several of Guru Gobind Singh's possessions. Besides jewelry and clothes there are his golden *kirpan,* two bows, a steel shield studded with gems, and five golden swords. The *gurdwara* also stables and cares for a horse that is said to be descended from the horse ridden by Guru Gobind Singh during his lifetime. The horse is led out for processions on special occasions. Throughout the year thousands of Sikh devotees visit this historical shrine on the banks of the Godavari River.

DAMDAMA SAHIB

Damdama Sahib is situated near Bhatinda in the Punjab just south of Amritsar. This *gurdwara* with its tranquil pool is sacred to the memory of Gobind Singh. The guru went there on the invitation of a devoted follower, Bhai Dalla, and liked the place so much that he stayed for more than nine months. His mirror, gun, and sword are displayed there.

Faith in the Khalsa

On a pillar at Takht Damdama Sahib are inscribed the words of Guru Gobind Singh expressing his firm faith in the Khalsa:

*To the Khalsa belongs all
My home, my body, and all that I possess.*

At Damdama Sahib Guru Gobind Singh pursued his literary work. There Bhai Mani Singh prepared the final version of the Guru Granth under the 10th guru's direction. The *gurdwara* became known as a seat of Sikh learning. It was even called the Guru's Kashi, after a famous center for Sanskritic and Hindu studies.

All Sikhs try to visit the five *takhts* at least once in their lifetime. Some make annual pilgrimages; others go only for special occasions. Some do not go to the *takhts* in person; instead they have continuous readings *(akhandpaths)* recited on their behalf. They also send money for the readers, for the kitchen, and for silk coverings for the holy book.

HISTORIC SHRINES AND PILGRIMAGE

Besides the Golden Temple and the five *takhts,* the Sikhs value many other *gurdwaras.* The birthplaces of the gurus and other sites also have special historical meaning. In the former princely state of Patiala, north of Delhi, two *gurdwaras*—Dukhniwaran Sahib in the city of Patiala and Bahadur Garh on its outskirts—are reminders of the ninth guru's visit. Sikhs travel there from all over the world. Visitors believe that a dip in the pool of Gurdwara Dukhniwaran Sahib will cure suffering—*dukhniwaran* literally means "the end of suffering" *(dukh).*

Such sacred places bring the past to life for Sikhs. Whenever they return to India Sikhs from America, Europe, the Middle East, and the Far East try to visit their historical shrines with their children, passing on the tradition. These Sikh centers of faith and history continue to inspire the Sikhs spiritually, intellectually, and politically.

SACRED TIMES

Sikhs try to bring their faith into their lives at all times. They do not view one time as being more sacred than another. Long ago

Bhatinda Fort

The *gurdwara* (Sikh place of worship) in the old fort in Bhatinda stands at the place where Guru Gobind Singh (1675–1708) stayed during a visit from Damdama Sahib. It was at this fort that Empress Razia Sultana (ca. 1250), the first woman ruler of India, was imprisoned before her execution. The *gurdwara* at the top of the fort is small and simple, but for Sikhs it is charged with historical significance.

Guru Nanak rejected the Indian custom of depending on astrology, the study of the heavenly bodies, to determine "good" days. "We remain busy counting and determining auspicious days," he said, "but we do not know that the Ultimate Reality is above and beyond such considerations."

However certain days of the month and of the year have an added element of festivity. The Sikhs inherited the ancient Indian lunar calendar based on the phases of the moon, so the new moon and the full moon are special for them. They incorporated the traditional Indian festivals into their year and gave them new meaning. They also added celebrations commemorating major events in Sikh history. Both the eternally returning seasons and the important and historic moments in Sikhism are celebrated with exuberance every year.

SANGRAND AND *MASIA*

In Western countries many Sikhs have adopted the custom of worshipping together on Sundays, but the opening, reading, and closing of the Guru Granth go on every day in people's homes and in the *gurdwaras. Gurdwaras* are open all the time and people come and go as they wish. Sikhs do not have a weekly holy day equivalent to the Jewish or Christian Sabbath. They do, however, regard the monthly *sangrand* and *masia* as special.

Sangrand is the first day of the month according to the Indian solar calendar. On this day Sikhs may add hopes and wishes for the coming weeks to their daily prayers. Many who do not regularly go to the *gurdwara* do so on this occasion. They pray for prosperity, health, and peace throughout the month. In the village *gurdwaras* warm *karahprasad* replaces the sugar puffs more commonly used for the sacrament.

Masia is the darkest night of the month. Many Sikhs think it is an especially good time for bathing in the holy pool of the *gurdwara*. The pool at Dukhniwaran Sahib in Patiala, for instance, is usually filled with devotees from all over the region. This tradition began at Tarn Taran near Amritsar and continues to be observed with great festival spirit. Around 10 at night a procession carries the Guru Granth from the Akal Takht to the *gurdwara* in Tam Taran. Sikh followers join in on the way, reciting hymns from the scripture. En route people serve simple meals and sweet snacks. The procession reaches the shrine at Tarn Taran in the early hours of the morning and everyone takes a dip in the holy pool. Sikhs feel that *sangrand* and *masia* celebrations help them to stay in harmony with the natural rhythms of the month.

BAISAKHI

Baisakhi is the first day of Baisakh, a month that is approximately equivalent to the month of April. Hindus in India traditionally celebrated this day at Hardwar, where the holy Ganges enters the plains. Guru Arjan began the Sikh tradition of Baisakhi celebrations at the Golden Temple. However even before that time Sikhs assembled during the month of harvest to thank the Ultimate and listen to the teachings of their gurus. In 1699 Guru Gobind Singh created the Khalsa on Baisakhi Day. For Sikhs this added special importance to the New Year celebration. Sikhs all over the world celebrate Baisakhi as a social, political, and religious occasion. The city of Amritsar, however, is a focal point in this annual event. Sikhs travel great distances to visit Harimandir, the Golden Temple, on this day. Singers and musicians perform throughout the day. The entire complex swarms with Sikh devotees bathing in the waters of the huge reflecting pool; listening to speakers and readers; preparing and consuming *langar,* the community meal that follows a service; making special offerings in the temple itself; and reverently circling the temple on the walkway as they contemplate and meditate.

The scene outside the Golden Temple complex is lively as well. For the large farming element in India Baisakhi is the last day to relax before the beginning of the harvest, so people make the most of it. They hold a large animal fair at which they buy and sell goats, buffaloes, camels, and other livestock.

Sikhs also recall the Baisakhi festival of 1919. On that date, fearing conspiracy, the British rulers had forbidden the people to gather. However many, including a large number of Sikhs, did

Young members of the Khalsa, wearing the five Ks, taking part in a procession to celebrate the Birthday of Guru Nanak in the city of Anandpur. The boys are wearing turbans to cover their uncut hair (under the turban, they will be wearing a *kanga* to keep their hair in place). They are wearing *kara,* a steel bangle, on their wrists and they are holding a *kirpan*, the sword. Under their robes, they will be wearing *kacchera,* short trousers to signify readiness to ride into battle.

gather in a small area near the Golden Temple called Jallianvala Bagh. The British fired on them and many hundreds, possibly over a thousand, died. Today political rallies take place at Jallianvala Bagh, where bullet holes from the massacre still scar the walls. Many who were not shot died trying to escape by jumping into deep wells, and these are still there as a terrible reminder.

DIVALI

Around the time of Christmas and Hanukkah in the West people in India celebrate Divali. Divali is a shortened form of the word *deepavali,* which literally means "a string of lights." For Hindus it is a major festival, welcoming the visit of the Lakshmi, the goddess of wealth and prosperity. It also commemorates the return of King Rama and Queen Sita to their kingdom of Ayodhya after 14 years of exile. In Sikhism, however, it is a reminder of the time when their sixth guru returned to Amritsar after the Mughal rulers released him from the fort of Gwalior. Guru Hargobind was falsely imprisoned by officers of Emperor Jahangir for nonpayment of fines imposed on his father. Furthermore his raising of an army had put him under suspicion of treason. However, after examining the case the emperor decided to release the guru.

At the Golden Temple Sikhs celebrate Divali for three days. Electric lights and earthenware oil lamps illuminate the central shrine, the walkways, and the adjoining building. Candles and lanterns float in the surrounding pool. Reflections of the temple lights merge with the floating lamps in a shimmering display. Fireworks light the night sky. Singers and musicians perform *kirtan,* the Sikh sacred music.

THE RELEASE OF GURU HARGOBIND SINGH

There were 52 Hindu princes in prison with Guru Hargobind Singh and the guru refused to leave unless his Hindu companions were set free also. According to tradition the emperor agreed, but on one condition. Only those princes could leave who could pass through a narrow passageway without losing hold of the guru's garments. Not to be outdone the guru ordered a cloak for himself made with long tassels hanging from it. The impossible was made possible: holding on to the tassels, all 52 princes walked to freedom. These same princes later betrayed the Guru Gobind, the 10th guru, and joined forces with the Mughal emperor. The battles that followed were responsible for a massacre that resulted in the deaths of Guru Gobind's two eldest sons and two of the five beloved Khalsa.

Fireworks, lamps, music, and pilgrimage to the Golden Temple are all part of joyful Divali celebrations which last for three days. Homes are also decorated with lanterns and candles and gifts exchanged between friends and family.

Speakers deliver lectures and recite heroic ballads. Sikhs offer gifts of cash, flowers, *karahprasad*, rice, butter, milk, and flour. Crowds come to view the Golden Temple's collection of precious jewels and to marvel at the golden gates, the golden canopy with its jeweled peacock, the pearl tassels, the golden fans, and the fly whisk made from millions of hairlike sandalwood fibers.

During Divali people whitewash and paint their homes and decorate them with earthenware lamps and candles. Families and friends exchange gifts and candy. For the Sikhs at this time, as for Hindus, Christians, and Jews around the world, the lights symbolize peace and joy.

BASANT

The festival Basant, is one which simply means "spring." During the time when the yellow mustard blooms in the Punjabi fields people wear yellow and eat yellow rice. In the villages of India the rooftops are full of youngsters flying kites. There are competitions to see whose kite will fly highest, but part of the fun is trying to sabotage other kites. The children attach bits of glass to their kites and try to cut their opponents' kite strings by flying across them. Basant is a colorful and festive time.

HOLA MOHALLA

Holi is a traditional spring festival of the Hindus. It celebrates the playful presence of the god. Lord Krishna. The festival occurs just as winter mellows into spring. During the Holi celebration people throw brightly colored paint and dye on one another. Friends and strangers alike are sprayed, splashed, and smeared with yellows, greens, reds, and blues. The scene in parks, streets, and shopping districts is one of vibrant color and merrymaking. Guru Gobind Singh gave this traditional spring festival a Sikh character. In Anandpur

he initiated the Hola Mohalla, a three-day festival during which Sikhs trained as soldiers. Although held at the same time as Holi, Hola Mohalla had a more serious purpose. What took place were contests in horsemanship, wrestling, and archery as well as mock battles and military exercises. The guru also encouraged competitions in music and poetry. Sikhs still celebrate the festival annually at Anandpur. They hold a large fair with singing, discussions, and athletic competitions.

Sikhs displaying martial arts skills at the festival of Hola Mohalla in Anandpur, Punjab. This three-day festival marks spring but there are also displays and contests of horsemanship, athletics, and military exercises.

RAKHRI

The festival of Rakhri comes in mid-August. A *rakhri* is a bright band that a sister ties around her brother's right wrist as she puts candy in his mouth. In turn the brother gives his sister a gift of money, clothes, or jewelry. This brief ritual symbolizes the bond between brother and sister. The sister prays for the long life and prosperity of her brother, and the brother promises to help and protect his sister whether she is single or married. Many Sikh families say Ardas, the basic prayer in which Sikhs remember their 10 gurus and the Guru Granth, before the tying of the *rakhri*. They may distribute *karahprasad* afterward.

GURPURABS

Gurpurabs are Sikh anniversaries. The birth dates of gurus, important historical events, and the martyrdom of Sikh heroes are remembered annually. After the new year begins in April, the first event in the Sikh calendar is the martyrdom of Guru Arjan. This falls in the month of Jaith, which corresponds to May–June in the Western calendar.

In August Sikhs celebrate the installation of the Guru Granth in the Golden Temple. As winter comes and Divali approaches

THE FESTIVALS OF SIKHISM	
April 13	Baisakhi
April	Birthday of Guru Tegh Bahadur
	Birthday of Guru Arjan
May	Birthday of Guru Angad
	Birthday of Guru Amar Das
May/June	Martyrdom of Guru Amar Arjan
June	Birthday of Guru Hargobind
July	Birthday of Guru Har Krishan
October/November	Divali
November	Birthday of Guru Nanak
November/December	Martyrdom of Guru Tegh Bahadur
December/January	Birthday of Guru Gobind Singh
March	Hola Mohalla

Sikhs celebrate the birthdays of the first and the 10th gurus, only a month apart. Guru Nanak's birthday falls in November. It is celebrated as the origin of the Sikh faith. This event is followed by Guru Gobind Singh's birthday in December. The martyrdom of the 10th guru's young sons also falls during December. It is preceded by the day of the martyrdom of Guru Tegh Bahadur.

GURPURABS IN THE UNITED STATES AND CANADA

Sikhs in places such as London, Hong Kong, Toronto, San Francisco, New York, and Washington, D.C., also celebrate the *gurpurabs*. Often they combine religious ceremonies with intellectual and cultural events. They invite musicians and lecturers from India and hold lavish *langars* and celebrations. They present seminars organized around Sikh themes in which both Sikhs and non-Sikhs may participate. They may organize plays, poetry readings, and performances of folk music from their heritage.

Sikhs celebrating a *gurpurab* with a parade and community celebrations in New York City.

During the various *gurpurabs* a float decorated with flowers carries the Guru Granth in a procession through the city or village. Sikhs recite scriptural hymns and serve *langar*. Wherever the procession goes people come out of their homes to see it. They cover their heads and remove their shoes to show homage to the holy book.

To commemorate *gurpurabs* people gather in the *gurdwaras*. Sikh scholars deliver lectures, and uninterrupted readings of the Guru Granth take place followed by *bhog* ceremonies in which worshippers say prayers and receive *karahprasad*. People also enjoy exhibits of Sikh treasures at shrines such as the Golden Temple.

Special customs are related to certain *gurpurabs*. Sikhs serve cold milk in water, a welcome refreshment in a hot month, on the anniversary of Guru Arjan's martyrdom. Arjan was tortured to death by being dipped in hot oil and sand and then thrown into cold waters. Sikhs also recall the martyrdom of Guru Gobind Singh's young sons in a special way. Zorowar Singh and Fateh Singh were bricked up behind a wall by rulers who wanted them to convert to Islam. The two boys held to their Sikh faith and died heroes. Millions gather each December in the Sirhind area of the Punjab to honor their memory. Farmers bring out wheat, grain, milk, and vegetables, and everyone shares enthusiastically in preparing and enjoying *langar*.

SACRED SPACE AND TIME

These festivals enable Sikhs to share in their heritage and keep the foundations of the community strong and lively. Such occasions help to deepen and enrich the Sikh experience, whether participants celebrate them by praying in a *gurdwara* or by simply participating in the festival atmosphere. For the Sikhs sacred space and sacred time are not two different or separate things. Rather they merge into the singular experience of the sacred that is beyond all space and time.

CHAPTER 8

WOMEN AND SIKHISM

From the beginning of Sikh tradition, women have held an important place. Sikh history holds stories of the many women who helped in many ways to shape the faith. Women have been active and central subjects in Sikh history and they are remembered in prayer and song along with their male counterparts.

Until Guru Nanak's time women in Indian society had long played a subordinate role. The inferior status of women, however, did not fit into the guru's vision of total equality for all people under the Universal Reality. Nanak declared:

Of woman are we born, of woman conceived,
To woman engaged, to woman married.
Woman we befriend, by woman do civilizations continue.
When a woman dies, a woman is sought for.
It is through woman that order is maintained.
Then why call her inferior from whom all great ones are born?
—From the Guru Granth

Sikh women and children gathered together during a marriage ceremony. By tradition, women sit separately from men in the *gurdwara*. Within the Sikh faith men and women are regarded as equal and women can lead the congregation in prayer, read the Guru Granth Sahib in the *gurdwara* and recite the sacred hymns.

Joti—the Divine Spark

The Ultimate Reality of Sikhism includes male and female alike. The Guru Granth affirms: "It itself is man; It itself is woman." The Sikh gurus expressed the Ultimate in feminine imagery. To identify the spark of Ultimate Reality within everyone, the gurus used the feminine noun *joti,* meaning "light." The insubstantial image of light helps to make both male and female Sikhs aware of the Ultimate within themselves.

The early gurus repudiated Indian customs that denied women an equal place in society. They spoke out against the Hindu custom of suttee, in which a widow had to sacrifice her own life at her husband's cremation. They dismissed the Islamic practice of *purdah,* whereby women had to veil their faces and bodies in public. And they rejected the custom of female infanticide, in which newborn girls, thought to be less valuable than boys, were put to death.

In some traditions women are regarded as "polluted," or unclean, for a part of each month and after childbirth. They may be barred from religious services during these times and required to undergo ritual cleansing before they can participate again. In Sikhism, however, women's bodies are considered whole and strong because of their function in giving birth. Women are the equals of men.

WOMEN IN THE SIKH COMMUNITY

To lead in worship, Sikhs choose people from within their *sangat,* or congregation. These leaders may be either women or men, as Sikhs consider members of both sexes equally endowed with moral and spiritual faculties. The third guru, Amar Das, established procedures that would ensure the participation of men and women in organizing and administering Sikh communities. Both men and women can read the Guru Granth. Both can recite *kirtan,* the sacred hymns. Both can officiate at any ceremony. In some branches of Sikhism the custom of turning to a guru for spiritual guidance has survived, but in general Sikhs make their own spiritual journeys guided by the Guru Granth.

WOMEN IN SIKH HISTORY

Although little is known about the women in Guru Nanak's life—his sister Nanaki, his mother Tripta, and his wife Sulakhni—many Sikhs believe that Nanak's message regarding equality of the sexes and his rejection of customs that were harmful to women were signs of their influence on him. Of special importance was Nanaki. She was five years older than Nanak, and the boy was named for her. Many clues suggest that she and her brother were very close. When Nanaki married and left home her brother went to live with her and her new family. She was the first to recognize his special gifts, and when others thought that Nanak had drowned in the River Bein Nanaki remained convinced that he was an immortal soul.

Sikh women and children gathered on the steps of their house in Anandpur, Punjab, to watch a festival parade to commemorate the birthday of Guru Nanak.

Other Sikh women, too, have been important to the Sikh faith. A few are described below.

MATA KHIVI

Mata Khivi was the wife of Angad, the second guru. The Guru Granth praises her warmth and generosity. Sikhs remember this outgoing woman, who died in 1582, for the feelings of affection and hospitality that she brought to the institution of *langar*. Under her liberal direction it became not just a symbolic meal but a real feast, with Mata Khivi supplying a delicious rice pudding. For her contributions to the tradition of *langar* Mata Khivi is described in the Guru Granth as "a thickly leafed tree" that brings shade and comfort to weary travelers. Sikhs also remember her as a wise adviser to her sons on spiritual and social matters.

BIBI BHANI

Bibi Bhani was the daughter of the third guru, Amar Das. She later married her father's successor, Guru Ram Das, and became the mother of Guru Arjan, the fifth guru, who compiled the Guru Granth. Sikhs remember Bibi Bhani as a strong woman with immense moral fervor. As the daughter, wife, and mother of gurus she had a profound influence. Guru Arjan's poetry contains a wealth of feminine images as if to underscore the importance of his mother's voice in his life. Bibi Bhani died in Taran Taran in 1598. In her memory Guru Arjan had a well built that provided water for refreshment and for agriculture, a fitting monument to her life.

MAI BHAGO

Mai Bhago was a courageous woman from the Amritsar district. During wartime, when a long siege had brought hardship to Anandpur, she rallied people who had fled that town and led them back to fight for Guru Gobind Singh. She herself took part in the battle at Muktsar on December 29, 1705, where she displayed courage and skill. Mai Bhago died in 1708. A monument to her memory stands at Hazur Sahib. The Sikh poet Bhai Vir Singh calls her a luminous star that provides light to all.

MATA GUJRI

Mata Gujri was born in 1627 and became the wife of Guru Tegh Bahadur. She was imprisoned in Sirhind with her two younger grandchildren, and all three died there as martyrs to the Sikh faith. Sikhs remember her especially for strengthening the faith of the young boys, who were sealed alive behind a brick wall and chose to die there rather than renounce Sikhism. The shrine of Joti Saroop marks the site where Mata Gujri was cremated on December 13, 1705. Her husband and two other grandsons also died as martyrs for the Sikh faith.

SADA KAUR

Sada Kaur was the mother-in-law of Maharaja Ranjit Singh, the first Sikh emperor. When he assumed the throne he was only 19, and he turned to his mother-in-law, whose counsel enabled him to unify the Punjab and create a Sikh state. She possessed great courage on the battlefield. The best part of her triumph, however,

MATA KAUR

When Guru Gobind Singh, the 10th guru, stirred the water of the first Khalsa initiation ceremony with his sword, his wife, Mata Sahib Kaur, added the sugar to the steel bowl. It was she who brought an element of celestial sweetness to the ritual. From that day on Khalsa members have traced their historical and spiritual beginnings to Guru Gobind Singh and Mata Sahib Kaur. The Khalsa members declare themselves to be the direct descendants of these two spiritual parents, who are equally important in the Khalsa family. Mata Sahib Kaur died in 1735.

Mata Sahib Kaur, the wife of Guru Gobind Singh at the first Khalsa initiation.

lay in peaceful victory. Under her direction and guidance Ranjit Singh was able to take control of the capital at Lahore without bloodshed. Sada Kaur also funded and administered Sikh institutions of learning. She died in Amritsar in 1832.

MAHARANI JINDAN

Maharani Jindan was born in 1817. She was married to Maharaja Ranjit Singh in 1835, toward the end of his life, and bore him a son, Dilip Singh, in 1837. The Maharaja died in 1839 and four years later six-year-old Dilip Singh succeeded him as leader of the Sikhs in the Punjab. Jindan, Dilip Singh's mother, became regent, or caretaker ruler, of the Sikh Empire. Maharani Jindan was famous for her keen intelligence. The British, then in power in India, found her a constant threat. Following an uprising in which the British put down the Khalsa, Jindan was accused of conspiracy and imprisoned. Her young son was taken to England and converted to Christianity. The Maharani continued to write powerful letters from prison. She later went to England and convinced her son to return to Sikhism. She died in England on August 1,1863.

WOMEN AND SIKH LITERATURE

Sikh literature contains women characters who display physical, intellectual, and spiritual strength. Two fictional heroines have been special favorites among the Sikh reading public—Sundari and Rani Raj Kaur, the creations of Bhai Vir Singh (1872–1957), a Sikh scholar, poet, and novelist.

SUNDARI—DEDICATION AND DARING

Sundari, first published about a hundred years ago, is the first novel in the Punjabi language and still the most acclaimed and widely read of all Sikh popular literature. Bhai Vir Singh began to write this novel when he was a young man—a student in high school. In this fast-paced adventure the young woman who is the main character is kidnapped by the Mughals, the Sikhs' traditional enemies. Rescued by a brother who has become a Sikh, she joins the Khalsa and takes the name Sundari. Within the Khalsa she lives according to the teachings of the guru and embodies the Sikh ideal.

The story of Sundari, with its vigorous action and high principles, captured the Sikh imagination as no other work of fiction ever had. Generations of Punjabi readers have been touched by Sundari's qualities of dedication, daring, and charity. The book has inspired many people to be initiated into the Khalsa.

RANA SURAT SINGH—THE JOURNEY OF A WISE RULER

Another of Bhai Vir Singh's works, *Rana Surat Singh,* published in 1905, gave Sikhs a second great fictional heroine. The five stages of spiritual ascension enumerated in the Jap, the first prayer of the Guru Granth, provide the framework for the book. In this epic the heroine, Rani Raj Kaur, makes a journey of faith, eventually realizing the highest stage of spiritual awareness. At the same time she moves in her daily life from a state of weakness and inaction to one of full participation in affairs of the world. Her spiritual experience gives her a new sense of self and a new orientation in the world, completely changing her domestic, social, and political life. At the end of the book Rani Raj Kaur assumes the political duties of her state and presides as a strong and wise ruler.

UNITY WITH THE UNIVERSE

From Rani Raj Kaur's story Sikhs take the message that the Sikh spiritual experience—the love for Ultimate Reality and the ascent into the sacred—is grounded in the love of fellow beings. The intimate relationships of the world—mother and daughter, sister and sister, husband and wife—are essential to the human condition. These relationships exist through the relationship of humans to the Ultimate Reality. For Sikhs the spiritual ascent has practical results. It helps them to recognize the fundamental unity of people and the universe.

CHAPTER 9

SIKH TRADITION AND MODERN CULTURE

Every religious tradition must face the demands of contemporary life if it is to survive and flourish. Sikhism has always encouraged its followers to participate fully in the political, social, and cultural climate in which they live. As Sikhism enters the new millennium it faces new challenges and opportunities in India and in the West.

THE RISE OF THE SIKH EMPIRE

After the death of the 10th Guru Gobind Singh in 1708 leadership fell to the Khalsa under Banda Singh Bahadur. For seven years he triumphed militarily over the Mughals, but was eventually captured, brutally tortured, and executed in 1716. With Banda's death the Khalsa withdrew to the hills in small bands. Decades of Mughal repression followed. However the Mughal Empire, once believed to be the greatest on earth, was steadily weakening due to invasions from Persia and then Afghanistan. In 1761 the Khalsa reestablished themselves as rulers over the region. Yet the

Khalsa Sikh soldiers taking part in a procession in Anandpur to celebrate Hola Mohalla. The soldiers display their traditioinal military skills and martial arts during the celebrations to honor Guru Gobind Singh.

Khalsa remained unstable, with bloody infighting characterizing the rest of the 18th century.

Stability would come from a new leader, Ranjit Singh. With the guidance of his mother-in-law, Sada Kaur, this teenage leader of a Khalsa band seized power peacefully in the city of Lahore in 1799. Over the next two years he carefully consolidated his strength, integrating 12 warrior Sikh bands into a sovereign state. On the day of Baisakhi, 1801, the Sikhs crowned him maharaja, or ruler king, of the Punjab.

Short of stature, dressed in white with the famous 240-carat Koh-i-noor ("mountain of light") diamond around his arm, and usually mounted on a horse, Ranjit Singh was a striking figure. Though illiterate, the "Lion of the Punjab" had the wisdom to surround himself with able servants from many countries. The maharaja was a skilled diplomat known for his prudence and deft ability to handle the increasingly powerful British, the Afghans, and the surrounding Indian princes. Under his reign culture and religion flourished. The first dictionary and grammar of the Punjabi language were printed, new *gurdwaras* were built and renovated, and many schools of North Indian painting flourished. By the time of his death in 1839 the Sikh Empire included Kangra, Multan, Kashmir, Derajat, Peshawar, Ladakh, and even Kabul.

THE DECLINE OF THE SIKH EMPIRE

Despite his personal charisma and military and diplomatic skills, Ranjit Singh failed to build a foundation that would secure the Sikh Empire after his death. Court intrigue claimed the lives of one son after another as family members battled one another in the hopes of ascending the throne. Ranjit Singh's leadership differed starkly with his sons' adoption of assassination and revenge. These destructive means of achieving power encouraged the repercussions that would soon destroy the young Sikh Empire. For while one son destroyed the next, the British were carefully planning to take over the entire region.

In 1845 the British set out to destroy the Sikh Empire. After four battles the Khalsa was defeated. It was an outcome the Sikhs

Border security controls at the Wagah border crossing between India and Pakistan about 17 miles (27 kilometers) from Amritsar. Because of the dramatic reduction in the Sikh population of Pakistan after Partition, many *gurdwaras* are no longer used and are in disrepair. Sikhs in Pakistan and beyond are trying to raise funds to restore these important historic *gurdwaras*.

would not accept. Three years later they rose up against the British and were victorious in their first clash. However the British armaments greatly outnumbered the Sikhs'. Despite valiant efforts they finally met with defeat in the Battle of Gujrat. On March 30, 1849, the British announced the complete annexation of Punjab. Maharaja Dalip Singh was forced to leave Punjab. His father's vast Empire was no more and the British now controlled most of the Indian subcontinent.

Under British domination Sikh morale reached its lowest point. Many Sikhs gave up Sikh practices and adopted those of the Hindus. By the census of 1868 the Sikhs, roughly estimated to number 10 million in Ranjit Singh's time, had dwindled to a little more than a million. The time was ripe for reform.

THE SINGH SABA AND BHAI VIR SINGH

In 1873 the first Singh Saba (Council) was formed in Amritsar, followed by the Lahore Saba in 1879. Others were subse-

RESURGENCE IN THE 20TH CENTURY

Bhai Vir Singh, the son of a Singh Saba founder, grew up close to the movement and devoted his entire life to the revival of Sikhism. The recipient of a Western education, Vir Singh studied English literature and history and used his studies to appraise his own Sikh heritage in a modern light. A prolific poet, writer, scholar, biographer of the gurus, and defender of the faith, he is the person most responsible for Sikhism's resurgence in the 20th century. Vir Singh's works of fiction, particularly the Punjabi classic *Sundari*, helped to explain the plight of the Sikh community, the goals of the reform movement, and the tangible ways of living the faith in the modern world.

quently founded throughout Punjab. Their mission was to return to the original message of the early gurus, to recover Sikh identity, but also to move the *panth,* or community, into the future. Through the Singh Sabas and their related institutions, un-Sikh practices such as worship of local gods, women's fasting for their husband's welfare, and the practice of astrology, were proscribed. Simultaneously many social and religious institutions were reformed. Schools, colleges, book clubs, educational societies, and printing presses were established to shape the minds and hearts of young Sikhs.

INDIAN INDEPENDENCE AND PARTITION

The modern world saw not merely the birth of colonialism, but movements of independence from the colonial powers. India's quest for *swaraj,* or self-rule, provides one of the noblest yet tragic stories of a nation's fight for freedom. Thousands of Indians dedicated themselves to the dream of an independent nation stretching from Kashmir in the north to Kanyakumari in the south.

After struggling for more than half a century India gained its independence on August 15, 1947. However it came at a high price. As the "Quit India" struggle had progressed in the 1920s and 1930s, Hindu and Muslim relations worsened. Increasingly Muslims believed that their interests would be best served by founding a new, separate nation. Ultimately the fear of a Hindu domination in an independent India led to the creation of Pakistan. Partition required that British India be divided into two new nations. The areas of the country with the greatest number of Muslims would constitute Pakistan, while the areas with the most Hindus would become India.

Of course areas were not always so easily divisible. So when partition came at the time of independence millions were forced to leave their homes and head either east or west to their new nation. The Sikhs were caught in the middle, for the line separating the new countries ran straight through Punjab The line of partition thus separated families, vocations, businesses, and *gurdwaras.* Rioting both preceded and followed the announcement of the new national boundaries. Hundreds of thousands of Sikhs were killed and millions of Punjabis were reduced to poverty, becoming India's new refugees as they left their homes in what was now the new state of Pakistan to seek a safer and more secure home in India. Perhaps one of partition's saddest ironies is that the Sikh community, the one most affected by the division of its Punjabi homeland, was ignored when the new boundaries were being determined.

SIKHISM TODAY

Partition did not end communal tensions in India, whose creation required uniting hundreds of factions representing different religious, cultural, racial, and ethnic groups. Much like the United States, India remains a democratic experiment. Although Sikhs created one of India's most prosperous states and comprise a sizable portion of India's professional and business people, they have not always been treated well by the Indian government. The powers in New Delhi tended to rule the *panth* inflexibly.

These and other conditions bred dissatisfaction and created pressure for home rule in Punjab beginning in the 1960s. The call for greater state of self-government was unwisely treated as a secessionist movement by the central government. The result was actually the strengthening of separatists who called for an independent Sikh nation known as Khalistan. While the separatists did not initially enjoy the support of most Sikhs, continuing government repression added to secessionist agitation. In 1983 Prime Minister Indira Gandhi's government dismantled the state government, administering affairs from the Indian capital in New Delhi.

ATTACK ON THE GOLDEN TEMPLE

Events reached a climax in 1984 when the Indian army fired on a group of separatists headquartered in the Golden Temple. Thousands of innocent Sikh civilians were killed and the Akal Takht was destroyed. This event represents the darkest chapter in modern Sikh history. Shortly after the attack on the Golden Temple

GROWTH AND INTERNATIONAL PARTNERSHIPS

Economic growth in India has also changed the priorities of the *panth,* or community. Sikhs are still dedicated to obtaining justice in India, but they are also concerned about schools for their children, the quality of their roads, and the health of Punjab's economy. The chief minister of Punjab now makes frequent visits to the United States and United Kingdom to enlist the financial support of successful American and British Sikhs and other nonresident Indians. These trips are yielding agreements for Punjabi development projects worth billions of dollars. Such projects reflect both the new willingness of India's central and state governments to tap into the resources of Indians around the globe, and the desire of successful nonresident Indians to improve the land of their birth.

World Sikhs

California is the U.S. state with the largest Sikh community; some 250,000 Sikhs live there with more than 50,000 in the San Francisco Bay area. The United States, Canada, and the United Kingdom are the countries with the largest Sikh populations outside India, although there are also sizable communities in Malaysia and Kenya.

and 11 other main *gurdwaras,* including Duk Navaran Shab in Patala, where thousands of innocent pilgrims were slaughtered, Prime Minister Indira Gandhi was assassinated by her two Sikh bodyguards. Reprisals throughout North India against innocent Sikhs quickly followed. It is estimated that in Delhi alone well over 3,000 people were killed during the four terrifying days following the assassination. Few of the perpetrators were brought to justice and it is widely believed that government and police officials allowed the violence to occur. Antagonism between Sikhs and Hindus had reached its apex in 1985.

ATTEMPTS TO DIFFUSE TENSIONS

Rajiv Gandhi, Indira Gandhi's son and successor as prime minister, recognized the danger of continued hostilities between Sikhs and Hindus, and that separatists reflected a minority within the entire Sikh population. Eager to defuse tensions, the prime minister signed an agreement with moderate Sikhs, promising to restore elections, to give Sikhs more economic and political power, and to recognize finally the Sikh religion in the Indian constitution. Hopes of a settlement or reconciliation were soon dashed when the Sikh signer of the Punjab Accord was assassinated, leaving the main political party leaderless. Rajiv Gandhi's administration backed away from the agreement, and the momentum toward reconciliation was well and truly lost.

Few could have predicted the way in which tensions would be eased between the Sikhs and the Indian government even two decades ago. For just as Rajiv Gandhi's administration was abandoning the Punjab Accord, it was also moving India in a new economic direction. As part of the central government's embrace of capitalism the state and central governments began seeking new trade and business partnerships outside the country. Economic liberalization is having a profound impact on India and thus on the Sikh community.

POLITICAL CHANGES

The 1990s brought significant political changes to India. In 1996, after more than four decades in power, the Congress Party was defeated in the Lok Sabha, India's lower house of parliament. Congress had led India to independence but it was now widely perceived as corrupt and ineffective. The Congress defeat came at the same time that the Bharatiya Janata Party (BJP) was gaining popularity. Dedicated to the vision of India as a uniquely Hindu nation, the BJP won a slim majority in the Lok Sabha in the 1996 election. The Shiromani Akali Dal, the Sikh political party, also benefited at the Congress Party's expense, with its members winning a majority of the Punjab seats in the Lok Sabha.

Both the BJP and the Shiromani Akali Dal quickly realized that an alliance promised to benefit both parties: the BJP could keep its majority in the Lok Sabha and the Shiromani Akali Dal could continue its rise to dominance in Punjab within the state and central governments. The alliance was formed shortly after the 1996 election. One year later the Shiromani Akali Dal won Punjab's state assembly elections with the help of the BJP. In 1998 their alliance swept the Lok Sabha seats in Punjab. In a relatively short time Sikh political fortunes had changed dramatically.

A SIKH PRIME MINISTER

The Shiromani Akali Dal led Punjab into the new century. However, many Sikhs questioned an alliance with the Hindu nationalists, fearing a return to the 1984 hostilities. This fear, the alliance's

lackluster governance, and the state's economic troubles led to its defeat by the Congress Party in the state assembly elections on February 13, 2002.

In May 2004 the Congress Party, led by Rajiv Gandhi's wife, Sonia Gandhi, won the biggest upset in India's political history by toppling the BJP. When Sonia Gandhi declined the prime minister post, Manmohan Singh, a Sikh, was sworn in as India's first minority prime minister, showing just how much had changed in two decades.

Indian prime minister Manmohan Singh meeting the former Russian prime minister, Victor Zubkov, during government talks in 2008. Taking his position as head of government in 2004, Manmohan Singh is the first Sikh to hold the office of Indian prime minister.

SIKHISM AS A GLOBAL FAITH

There was a time when the Sikh story ended at the borders of the Indian subcontinent, but that time is past. Due to emigration in the last century the *panth* can now be found in such disparate places as New Zealand, Fiji, England, Canada, and the United States. Sikhism's presence in the United States and Canada began in the late 1800s.

THE FIRST SIKHS IN AMERICA

One of the lesser-known stories of Sikh emigration occurred in California. Attracted by fertile farmland resembling Punjab, Sikhs founded communities in California's Central and Imperial valleys. As in Punjab their dedication was rewarded with thriving farms and businesses. By 1920 Punjabis owned or leased one-third of all Imperial Valley farmland. Such success was met with fear and prejudice by the Americans of the time. Restrictive laws were enacted to keep Punjabis out of the United States. In 1901 a California law was adopted prohibiting the marriage of nonwhite people to Anglos. One newspaper in the Imperial Valley ran a headline reading "Hindu Invasion," reflecting a basic ignorance of the Sikh faith. Unfortunately such ignorance was repeated a century later.

In 1917 new federal immigration laws were adopted that actually revoked the citizenship of Indians and other Asians already well established in the United States. Sikhs proudly fought such unjust laws. Bhagat Singh Thind, a naturalized American citizen who fought for the United States in World War I (1914–1918), challenged the new anti-Asian immigration law all the way to the Supreme Court but lost his case. In 1923 he was stripped of his citizenship. It was not restored until 1946 under the Filipino and Indian Naturalization Act.

As the 20th century progressed Americans became increasingly aware of racial prejudice in their own country and its influence on immigration policy. The Immigration and Naturalization Act of 1965 finally ended the long history of racial prejudice in American immigration law. Sikh immigration was not immediate, however. Sikhs only began arriving in record numbers after

Sandeep Singh, age 5, of Cherry Hill, New Jersey, watches as a float passes by during the annual Sikh Day Parade in April 2002 in New York. The parade, which has been a tradition since 1987, runs down Broadway from Times Square to Madison Square Park.

the 1984 attack on the Golden Temple. Since then thousands of Sikh faithful have moved to the United States. Sikh *gurdwaras* can now be found in places such as Somerville, Massachusetts; Chicago, Illinois; Garland, Texas; and San Diego, California.

THE SIKH COALITION

On January 1, 2000, the world ushered in the new millennium. However, in many ways the terrorist attacks on the United States on September 11, 2001, marked the true beginning of a new epoch. On that day terrorists of Arabic descent attacked New York City and Washington, D.C., claiming to be motivated by their Islamic faith. The events of that day were to affect the Sikh community deeply.

Around the country, and indeed in many parts of the world, misguided people targeted Sikhs as Arabs. Some Sikhs were even killed. The first reaction of the communities was a mixture of shock, fear, and disbelief. Like their countrymen, Sikh Americans mourned for the innocent victims of the terrorist attacks, but they also mourned for the crimes done to the Sikh community by their fellow citizens. It was not long, however, until the *panth* mobilized to defend the rights not just of Sikhs but all minorities. Today groups like the Sikh Coalition are working to safeguard civil rights and to educate the general public about the Sikh faith. Indeed many *gurdwaras* are now engaged in educational outreach to their cities and towns.

MAINTAINING IDENTITY

While innovations like Sikh Web sites are helpful, Sikh communities are finding that the young growing up in areas where Sikhism is not the dominant social force find it hard to maintain their sense of identity. Young men in particular often cut off their long hair and no longer wear the turban because they wish to assimilate. However events such as the mistakes made after 9/11 and the rise of a stronger awareness of and pride in Sikh culture often change these attitudes. In the United Kingdom, for example, the success of a Sikh cricketer on the England team helped many young Sikhs feel a sense of pride in their tradition. In the United States there is a significant annual festival—the Festival of Sikh Films in the Western World—that brings together young, enterprising Sikhs who explore together their own roles in the West.

In the Punjab economic depression and, sadly, corruption at the government level has led to the breakdown of many Sikh families and the rise of drug addiction and alcoholism—both strictly forbidden by Sikh teachings. The community is now reaching out to these people, helping them to recover their sense of pride.

A HOPEFUL VISION

Being a Sikh in the contemporary world is not easy, but the ideals of Sikhism still guide the communities, and Sikhs are looking more to the profound spiritual truths and less to the cultural accretions that have marked Sikhism as essentially an ethnic religion rather than a universal one. There are so called White Sikhs, converts who follow a specific guru, but Sikhism has yet to break out of its historical and cultural constraints and become the world religion that many feel it has the potential to become.

Sikhism developed in a sea of tumult. Yet throughout its history the faith has managed to survive and even flourish. Sikhism's strong work ethic, value system, and stress on community win its members both respect and success. To a world dominated by violence Sikhism teaches peace, equality, and service. To a world often consumed by materialism and selfishness Sikhism offers the path of heightened awareness of other people, the natural rhythms of nature, and the past. And to a world fractured by human division of all kinds Sikhism stresses common humanity. Indeed the Sikh ideals of unity, equality, honesty, and service provide a hopeful vision for the world of the present and the future.

FACT FILE

Worldwide Numbers

There are 24 million members of the Sikh faith, the majority of whom live in India. There are large Sikh populations in the United States, Canada, Great Britain, Pakistan, East Africa, and Malaysia.

Holy Symbol

In the center is two-edged sword, which is used to prepare food during services. Around this is a circle symbolizing one God with no beginning or end. On the outside are two swords that are said to represent the defense of justice and truth.

Founders

The first guru of the Sikh faith was Guru Nanak. He was followed in turn by another nine gurus.

Holy Places

The main site for Sikh pilgrimage is the city of Amritsar with the Golden Temple, which was built by the successor to the fourth guru.

Holy Writings

The main text is called the Guru Granth Sahib. It contains hymns written by some of the gurus, and it is seen by many Sikhs as the living guru. It also contains some writings from Hindu and Muslim writers. In many *gurdwara* and homes a copy of the Guru Granth Sahib is kept in a room of its own. Many people refer to the Guru Granth Sahib for inspiration and it is read from start to finish at Sikh festivals.

Festivals

There are four main festivals in the Sikh faith: Divali, the festival of lights, which celebrates the release of the sixth guru from prison (October/ November); Hola Mohalla is the spring festival of colors and sportsmanship (March); Baisakhi, which celebrates the New Year; and Rakhri, for children (mid-August). Gurpurbs are festivals that celebrate the gurus.

BIBLIOGRAPHY

Jogendra Singh, and Gurdial Singh Man. *Sikh Ceremonies*. Ludhiana: Lahore Book Shop, 1999.

Kapur Singh, Piara Singha, and Madanjit Kaur. *Parasaraprasna: The Baisakhi of Guru Gobind Singh*. Amritsar: Guru Nanak Dev University, 2001.

Shri Guru Granth Sahib. Internet Sacred Text Archive. Available online. URL: http://www.sacred-texts.com/skh/granth/index.htm. Accessed November 21, 2008.

The Pluralism Project at Harvard University. Available online. URL: http://www.pluralism.org/resources/statistics/tradition.php#Sikhism. Population of Sikhs in U.S. Accessed December 15, 2008.

FURTHER READING

Cole, W. Owen, and Piara Singh Sambhi. *The Sikhs: Their Religious Beliefs and Practices.* Brighton: Sussex Acad. Press, 2006.

Daljeet Singh, and Angela Smith. *The Sikh World.* Morristown, N.J.: Silver Burdett Co, 1985.

Goswami, Sandeep, and Malkiat Singh. *The Great Glory: Sikhism.* New Delhi: Rupa & Co, 2006.

Grewal, J.S. *Contesting Interpretations of the Sikh Tradition.* Delhi: Manohar Publishers, 1998.

McLeod, W. H. *Exploring Sikhism: Aspects of Sikh Identity, Culture and Thought.* Oxford India paperbacks. New Delhi: Oxford University Press, 2003.

———. *Historical dictionaries of religions, philosophies, and movements, no. 59.* Lanham, Md: Scarecrow Press, 2005.

———. ed. and trans. *Textual Sources for the Study of Sikhism.* Chicago: University of Chicago Press, 1990.

———. *The Sikhs: History, Religion and Society.* New York: Columbia University Press, 1989.

Singh, Harbans. *The Heritage of the Sikhs,* 2nd ed. Delhi: Manohar Publishers, 1994.

Singh, Nikki-Guninder Kaur. *The Name of My Beloved: Verses of the Sikh Gurus.* India: Penguin, 2001.

Singh, Patwant. *The Sikhs.* New York: Alfred E Knopf, 2000.

Wolpert, Stanley. *A New History of India,* 6th ed. New York: Oxford University Press, 1999.

WEB SITES

Further facts and figures, history, and current status of the religion can be found on the following Web sites:

http://www.allaboutsikhs.com
A comprehensive Web site on Sikhism, Sikh history and philosophy, customs and rituals, Sikh way of life, social and religious movements, art, and architecture.

http://www.sikhs.org
A view on the philosophy, development, and way of life of Sikhism.

http://www.sikhpoint.com
A network for Sikhs of all ages around the world to share their beliefs, customs, thoughts, and ideas. Its main functions are education and community projects.

http://sikhchic.com
A team of Sikh specialists provide information on all aspects of Sikhism. There is also information on Sikh art, architecture, music, literature, and culture.

GLOSSARY

amrita—Nectar of immortality.

anand karaj—Literally, "blissful occasion." The Sikh marriage ceremony, constituting both religious and legal aspects of the marriage.

Ardas—The prayer that forms the culmination of the Sikh service.

Baisakhi—The Sikh New Year's Day, a festival that takes place in April and celebrates the founding of the Khalsa.

dharam—Moral duty; the first stage of spiritual ascension as recorded in the Jap.

Divali—The Sikh Festival of Lights, celebrated in October or November.

granthis—Readers of the Guru Granth during Sikh worship.

gurpurabs—Anniversary celebrations commemorating gurus' birth dates, the martyrdom of Sikhs, and historical events.

Guru Granth—In Sikhism, the sacred text that contains the compositions of the Sikh gurus, as well as those of Hindu and Muslim saints, and forms the center of all Sikh ceremony and ritual; also known as Adi Granth—literally, "first book"—the first title given to the Guru Granth.

gurdwara—Literally, "door to enlightenment." The Sikh place of worship.

gyan—Literally, "knowledge." The second stage of spiritual ascension as recorded in the Jap.

Harimandir—The House of God. Harimandir is the central shrine of the Sikhs, built by Arjan, the fifth guru, and located in Amritsar, India. Because its exterior appears to be covered with gold, it is called the Golden Temple.

Jap—The morning prayer of the Sikhs. The Jap forms the beginning of the Guru Granth and presents the foundation of Sikh philosophy and doctrine.

karahprasad—The Sikh sacrament. Made of equal amounts of flour, sugar, water, and butter, this sweet mixture is placed in the cupped palms of the members of the congregation at the end of the Sikh service.

Kaur—Literally, "princess." The second name given to all Sikh women.

Khalsa—Literally, "pure ones." The fellowship of Sikhs founded by Gobind Singh, the 10th guru, on Baisakhi in 1699.

khanda—The double-edged sword used as a symbol of Sikhism.

kirtan—The singing of hymns, an important part of Sikh service. Verses from the Guru Granth are sung in the appropriate musical measures, often accompanied by such instruments as the harmonium and the tabla (drums).

langar—The community kitchen. In Sikh shrines and during Sikh gatherings men and women cook meals and, sitting in rows on the floor, eat together, regardless of race and caste.

Mul Mantra—The short passage that begins the Guru Granth; Sikhism's essential creed describing the Oneness of Reality and Its transcendent nature.

panj pyare—Literally, the "five beloved." The name given to the five Sikhs who were prepared to give their life for their faith; the first five members of the Khalsa.

Punjab—The fertile farming region in northwestern India that is home to the Sikhs; literally, "five rivers" because of its relationship to the Indus River and its five tributaries.

sangat—Gathering or congregation.

Sat Sri Akal—Literally, "Truth is the Timeless One." The Sikh greeting, said while pressing one's palms together and gently bowing.

Singh—Literally, "lionhearted." The second name of all Sikh men, first used by Guru Gobind Singh to eliminate the caste distinctions and to instill heroism in his people.

Wahe Guru—Literally, "Wonderful Guru." The expression is equivalent to saying "Amen," "Cheers," "Bon Appetit," and "God Bless You," and it is pronounced before and after any major or minor undertaking.

INDEX

ABOUT THE AUTHOR

Nikky-Guninder Kaur Singh is the Crawford Family Professor of Religion and former department chair at Colby College in Waterville, Maine. She has published extensively in the field of Sikhism.

ABOUT THE SERIES EDITORS

Martin Palmer is the founder of ICOREC (International Consultancy on Religion, Education, and Culture) in 1983 and is the secretary-general of the Alliance of Religions and Conservation (ARC). He is the author of many books on world religions.

Joanne O'Brien has an M.A. degree in Theology and has written a range of educational and general reference books on religion and contemporary culture. She is co-author, with Martin Palmer and Elizabeth Breuilly, of *Religions of the World* and *Festivals of the World* published by Facts On File Inc.

PICTURE CREDITS